PREDATORY
PRICING

ORGANISATION FOR ECONOMIC CO-OPERATION AND DEVELOPMENT

Pursuant to article 1 of the Convention signed in Paris on 14th December 1960, and which came into force on 30th September 1961, the Organisation for Economic Co-operation and Development (OECD) shall promote policies designed:

- to achieve the highest sustainable economic growth and employment and a rising standard of living in Member countries, while maintaining financial stability, and thus to contribute to the development of the world economy;
- to contribute to sound economic expansion in Member as well as non-member countries in the process of economic development; and
- to contribute to the expansion of world trade on a multilateral, non-discriminatory basis in accordance with international obligations.

The original Member countries of the OECD are Austria, Belgium, Canada, Denmark, France, the Federal Republic of Germany, Greece, Iceland, Ireland, Italy, Luxembourg, the Netherlands, Norway, Portugal, Spain, Sweden, Switzerland, Turkey, the United Kingdom and the United States. The following countries acceded subsequently through accession at the dates indicated hereafter: Japan (28th April 1964), Finland (28th January 1969), Australia (7th June 1971) and New Zealand (29th May 1973).

The Socialist Federal Republic of Yugoslavia takes part in some of the work of the OECD (agreement of 28th October 1961).

Publié en français sous le titre:

PRIX D'ÉVICTION

This report covers predatory pricing, pricing so low that competitors quit rather than compete, permitting the predator to raise prices in the long run. Predatory pricing is subject to the competition laws and policies of most OECD countries, but there has been a lively controversy over what standards should be applied. Some officials go so far as to urge that any rule against predation will do more harm than good by depriving consumers of the benefits of vigorous price competition.

This report examines the conflicting proposals for a standard to control predatory pricing and recommends a method of analysis which competition officials should follow. Major emphasis is given to identifying when low pricing should not be of concern to competition authorities.

Also available

COMPETITION POLICY AND INTELLECTUAL PROPERTY RIGHTS (May 1989)
(24 89 03 1) ISBN 92-64-13242-2   136 pages   £11.00   US$19.00   FF90.00   DM37.00

DEREGULATION AND AIRLINE COMPETITION (June 1988)
(24 88 02 1) ISBN 92-64-13101-9   168 pages   £12.00   US$22.00   FF100.00   DM43.00

INTERNATIONAL MERGERS AND COMPETITION POLICY (December 1988) bilingual
(24 88 03 3) ISBN 92-64-03143-X   115 pages   £11.00   US$20.00   FF90.00   DM39.00

THE COSTS OF RESTRICTING IMPORTS: The Automobile Industry (January 1988)
(24 87 06 1) ISBN 92-64-13037-3   174 pages   £8.50   US$18.00   FF85.00   DM36.00

COMPETITION POLICY AND JOINT VENTURES (February 1987)
(24 86 03 1) ISBN 92-64-12898-0   112 pages   £6.50   US$13.00   FF65.00   DM29.00

COMPETITION POLICY IN OECD COUNTRIES:

    1987-1988 (February 1989)
    (24 89 01 1) ISBN 92-64-13192-2   294 pages   £19.50   US$34.00   FF160.00   DM66.00

    1986-1987 (May 1988)
    (24 88 01 1) ISBN 92-64-13075-6   284 pages   £15.00   US$27.50   FF125.00   DM54.00

    1985-1986 (October 1987)
    (24 87 04 1) ISBN 92-64-12970-7   272 pages   £8.00   US$17.00   FF80.00   DM34.00

COMPETITION POLICY AND THE PROFESSIONS (February 1985)
(24 85 01 1) ISBN 92-64-12685-6   112 pages   £7.50   US$15.00   FF75.00   DM33.00

MERGER POLICIES AND RECENT TRENDS IN MERGERS (October 1984)
(24 84 06 1) ISBN 92-64-12624-4   122 pages   £6.30   US$13.00   FF63.00   DM28.00

COMPETITION AND TRADE POLICIES. Their Interaction (October 1984)
(24 84 05 1) ISBN 92-64-12625-2   154 pages   £6.00   US$12.00   FF60.00   DM27.00

COMPETITION LAW ENFORCEMENT. International Co-operation in the Collection of Information (March 1984)
(24 84 01 1) ISBN 92-64-12553-1   126 pages   £6.00   US$12.00   FF60.00   DM27.00

Prices charged at the OECD Bookshop.

*THE OECD CATALOGUE OF PUBLICATIONS and supplements will be sent free of charge
on request addressed either to OECD Publications Service,
2, rue André-Pascal, 75775 PARIS CEDEX 16, or to the OECD Distributor in your country.*

TABLE OF CONTENTS

I. INTRODUCTION

The subject of predatory conduct, predatory pricing in particular, is topical again. Several trends have converged which make an examination of predation timely. The first is the sweeping movement throughout the OECD to increase competition and efficiency through the deregulation of numerous sectors and the privatisation of state-owned enterprises. This movement raises concerns that the newly freed firms, often dominant in their markets, will seek unfairly to protect their positions against new entrants. Second, there is the increasingly difficult area of international trade, where economic dislocations in connection with rising imports have caused many domestic industries to charge their foreign competitors with dumping. This increasing concern over international trading practices could benefit from clear thinking about what pricing should be considered predatory.

The economic literature on predatory pricing has likewise been in a state of flux. Although early theorists made intuitive arguments on the dangers of predation, this view has been largely displaced by theories that price predation is irrational and should therefore be rare. While this latter view has become the conventional wisdom affecting the formation of pricing rules and decisions by courts and competition policy officials, still more recent theories have cropped up arguing that predatory pricing can indeed be rational in certain circumstances. To the extent that these newer views are correct, heightened concern over predation is warranted.

Another recent phenomenon is the emergence of concern over non-price predation. Non-price predation, sometimes called raising rivals' costs, includes the abuse of judicial and administrative procedures to impede domestic and foreign competitors. Because the rules against predatory pricing and dumping are natural weapons for the non-price predator, it is important that these rules be no broader than necessary; rules which are overbroad or imprecise invite their abuse for anticompetitive purposes.

Non-price predation is not the only reason why predatory pricing rules must be carefully drawn; an imprecise rule carries real risks of costly errors. Mistaking competitive pricing as predatory will tend to inhibit price competition in the economy. On the other hand, mistaking predation for competition may foster higher prices from increased concentration in the long run. In light of these considerations, competition authorities should not take action unless the existence of predatory pricing can be established with a reasonable degree of accuracy and should recognize that it may be better to have no explicit rule prohibiting predatory pricing than to mechanically enforce such a rule.

Rules of one type or another concerning predatory conduct are found in the competition laws and policies of most Member countries. These rules typically prohibit abuse of dominant position, efforts to monopolize a market or price discrimination to injure competition in a market. In addition, a few Member countries have particular legislation prohibiting sales below some cost floor, generally without reference to the market power of the firm or the effect of the practice on competition. These sale-at-a-loss prohibitions are described even though they might not normally be considered to be predation rules. They could, nonetheless, operate in the same fashion as a cost-based anti-predation rule. Thus, any lessons drawn from examining the latter type rules could illuminate the former. In addition, provisions relating to "loss-leader" and advertised but unavailable items exist in some Member countries but are not examined in this report. Provisions of this type are as often found under consumer protection regimes as they are under competition policy, and thus go beyond the scope of the present study. This report describes briefly the legal framework in each Member country as well as significant cases arising under those laws. It should be kept in mind, however, that a number of Member countries report that no such cases have yet arisen under their laws. In addition, a number of necessary elements in the treatment of a predatory pricing case are beyond the scope of this report. For example, questions concerning market definition and what constitutes a dominant position or market power are not examined.

This report defines predation as short-run conduct which seeks to exclude rivals on a basis other than efficiency in order to protect or acquire market power. Such exclusion can be attempted through short-run pricing so low as to induce exit or deter entry, or through non-price conduct which can, in addition, put rivals at a disadvantage by raising their costs. Longer run entry-deterring conduct such as limit pricing is not within the scope of this report. This report discusses the theories of both price and non-price predation, but its primary emphasis will be on the former as the evolution of legal rules governing predatory pricing has been the subject of considerable controversy in recent years.

The academic debate over the appropriate predatory pricing rule is reflected in several ways in this report. First, a chapter is given over to a presentation of the major proposals. Second, an effort is made in the discussion of the case law to uncover to what extent the various proposals have been accepted or rejected by courts and competition policy officials. This case law discussion shows, moreover, how antitrust concepts circulate internationally. In particular, proposals generated in the American academic debate over predatory pricing rules have begun to find their way into competition law decisions of other Member countries. For example, in a recent decision in the European Community, the defendant, a Dutch firm, argued that its pricing should not be seen as an abuse of dominant position given the reasoning of Areeda and Turner, authors of an influential article which appeared in the Harvard Law Review. Thus, the academic debate should be of interest to competition policy officials and practitioners in each Member country.

The organisation of the report is as follows: Chapter 2 presents the theories of price and non-price predation. Chapter 3 discusses the available information on the prevalence of predatory pricing. Chapter 4 presents the major proposals to govern predatory pricing which have emerged in the past decade. Chapter 5 identifies the legal basis to control predatory pricing in Member countries while Chapter 6 examines the application of those laws and competition policies in concrete situations. Finally, Chapter 7 presents conclusions and suggestions for the analysis of claims of predatory pricing.

II. THE ECONOMICS OF PREDATION

A. Predatory pricing

The traditional theory of predatory pricing is straightforward. The predator, already a dominant firm, sets its prices so low for a sufficient period of time that its competitors leave the market and others are deterred from entering. Assuming that the predator and its victims are equally efficient firms, this implies that the predator as well as its victims has incurred losses and that these losses are significant. For the predation to be rational, there must be some expectation that these present losses (or foregone profits), like any investment, will be made up by future gains. This in turn implies that the firm has some reasonable expectation of gaining exploitable market power following the predatory episode, and that profits of this later period will be sufficiently great to warrant incurring present losses or foregoing present profits. The theory also implies that some method exists for the predator to outlast its victim(s), whether through greater cash reserves, better financing or cross-subsidisation from other markets or other products.

This traditional view was later supplemented by an argument that the potential benefits to the predator were not limited to future gains in the market where it predated. The predatory campaign could be seen as an investment in reputation which could pay dividends in other geographic or product markets by deterring entry or disciplining rivals[1]. These spillover effects thus would multiply the gains from the initial predatory episode. Scherer refers to it as:

> "... the demonstration effect that sharp price cutting in one market can have on the behaviour of actual or would be rivals in other markets. If rivals come to fear from a multimarket seller's actions in Market A that entry or expansion in Markets B and C will be met by sharp price cuts or other rapacious responses, they may be deterred from taking aggressive actions there. Then the conglomerate's expected benefit from predation in Market A will be supplemented by the discounted present value of the competition-inhibiting effects its example has in Markets B and C."[2]

It has also been argued that the threat to predate could be made even more credible if the dominant firm increased its investment, e.g. in plant capacity, before entry. By increasing its non-recoverable or "sunk" costs, the predator demonstrates its commitment to fight. Further, if the minimum efficient scale is large relative to the overall market, the predator's "strategic" investment could ensure that an additional minimum efficient scale plant would cause sufficient excess capacity to drive prices down to an unremunerative level.

The theory of predation set out above came under strong attack by a number of writers including Areeda, McGee[3] and Easterbrook[4]. McGee argues that predation is more costly to the predator than the victim, given the predator's larger market share, and that as the campaign and market share increase, so too do the costs. Against these large and certain costs are future profits which must be discounted in two ways, once to reduce them to present value terms and then again to reflect the uncertainty that they will arise. He then gives reasons why the future monopoly profits might not be realised: the prey might enter into long-term contracts with customers (who would not want to see a competing supplier disappear), find financing to ride out the price cutting or shut down and wait for prices to rise. Even if the victim does go out of business, new entry is possible in the post-predation period (the existence of the victim demonstrates that entry is possible[5]. Most important, however, is McGee's point that the threat of predation is not credible because it would not pay to carry it out; the dominant firm would lose more by predating than by co-existing with a rival[6].

McGee further argues that better monopolising strategies exist. He finds that mergers to monopoly, where legal, would make more sense to the dominant firm, as mergers would avoid the large losses to the dominant firm of a predatory campaign. Given these losses, he doubts that a predatory campaign could lower acquisition costs sufficiently, believing that the losses to the predator will be even greater than the savings generated[7].

Easterbrook covers much the same ground as McGee but with differing emphasis and greater elaboration of a number of points. In particular he argues that the victim should have a variety of sources of aid either through the capital markets or through being acquired by its own financially strong backer. Customers of the victim should also help:

> "The point is this: as long as victims and customers have rational expectations about the future conduct of predators, and the predators themselves behave rationally, the intended victim should always be able to offer some package that is more attractive to customers than the monopolist's offer of low prices followed by monopoly prices. Potential predators will understand that victims can make these responses, and thus they will not make predatory threats."[8]

Easterbrook further makes a lengthy demonstration of the unfavourable mathematics of a predatory campaign, noting that both present losses and foregone present profits must be earned back by monopoly profits and that, given discount rates and the uncertainty of those profits, predation seemed unlikely to be profitable[9].

Easterbrook also discusses the possibility that predation in one market could be used to create a reputation in other markets — that predation is a signal to competitors and potential entrants in other markets not to enter or compete vigorously. He finds the argument not persuasive, however, because the original threat to predate is not credible. He cites the example of a monopolist with ten markets to defend who predates in market 1 to signal his willingness to protect markets 2 to 10. The potential entrants realise that while predation would not pay to defend a single market, it would pay and therefore be put into operation to protect several markets. Thus, the expectation would be that the predator, having "sunk" predatory costs once in market 1, would be willing to do so again in market 2 to protect markets 3 to 10. Easterbrook points out, however, that potential entrants could see through this threat. First the potential entrants would look to the last (tenth) market to be entered and see that predation would not pay in that market. Predation would not pay because there would be no more markets to protect; all the other markets have already been predated. With the predator having nothing to gain from the protection of other markets, the entrants can see that the predator would be better off by sharing that last market rather than by waging a costly predatory campaign. Therefore the potential entrants conclude that predation would not be enacted in the tenth market. The potential entrants then focus on the ninth market. This market is now effectively the last market, and the potential entrants see that the predator again would find it more profitable to co-exist than fight. This reasoning can continue market-by-market back to market 1. Thus, the predatory signal has "unraveled" and, because it would not deter, it would not be implemented.[10]

Easterbrook and McGee apply similar logic to dismiss the possibility that the predator will engage in strategic capacity expansion. They argue that, like predation, the threat is not credible because it would not pay to carry it out; even if the plant were built, the predator would be better off accommodating the new entrant by restricting output and maintaining prices rather than by maintaining pre-entry output. While the entrant would lose money if output were maintained, the predator would, having greater market share, lose still more. Because the predator *and* the potential entrant would know this, the entrant would not be deterred from entry. Knowing that the entrant would reason in that fashion, the predator might not build excess plant.

A second point is that if the potential entrant can create long-term contracts with buyers before entry (theoretically it should be able to underbid the pre-entry limit price), it could weather the storm of excess capacity generated by price cutting after entry[11].

Easterbrook's criticism of the credibility of a threat to predate in multiple markets follows from work by Selten, who used game theory to demonstrate how rational players could unravel threats of predation in multiple markets[12]. Selten called the result of this reasoning the "Chain Store Paradox" because people seem to believe intuitively that predation should pay while the logic of game theory says it shouldn't. Further, the payoff to the predatory chain store in his game is greater if the store and the entrants believe in the predatory threat and act accordingly. Selten finds the intuitive result to be the more convincing explanation of how people will respond to the chain store situation[13]. He suggests that the type of abstract thinking required to find the game theory solution to the problem is unlikely to occur in real-life situations[14].

Later writers resolve Selten's paradox by showing that the logic of his game theory holds only for multiple markets with perfect information, that is, each potential entrant *knows* that it is not in the interest of the monopolist to fight. For example, Milgrom and Roberts present a model assuming, as McGee does, that predation is irrational in a single market. They also assume multiple markets, multiple entrants and some uncertainty on behalf of each entrant as to the benefits to the monopolist from an aggressive response to entry i.e., is the monopolist pricing low because it is predating or does it simply have lower costs[15]? Now the entrants cannot look to the last market and see that low pricing would be against the monopolist's interests; a monopolist with a cost advantage might well use it even in the last market. With information thus imperfect, entrants will then base their expectations about future predation on past conduct, giving the established firm an incentive to build a reputation as a predator[16]. They conclude:

"The implications of this analysis for antitrust policy are straightforward. In multiple market situations, predation can be a rational strategy which deters entry and thus supports monopoly. Thus, any tendency to discount the likelihood or significance of predation on the basis of its presumed irrationality should be checked when there are multiple markets which might reasonably be regarded by potential entrants as similar ... Firms serving several geographically distinct markets are only one case where the model and its conclusions might apply. Firms with broad product lines or those in which on-going technological change yields a pattern of new product introduction over time are others. In this context, it is worth noting explicitly that predation will only rarely need to be practised. The credible threat of predation will deter all but the toughest entrants ... and so the occasions when the firm will be called upon to carry out its threat will be infrequent."[17]

Easterbrook has recognised that his model of the irrationality of predation assumes that each firm knows the others' costs and strategies, and that the analysis becomes less clear when imperfect information is introduced. He argues, however, that because the predator has similarly imperfect information as the prey, each side is equally handicapped and neither has a superior strategy[18].

Intuitively, though, it would seem that an established firm should have better information about costs, including the likely costs of a new firm, than the new entrant would have about the costs of the established firm, assuming similar process and product technologies. The presence of a significant learning curve may also make the evolution of costs clearer to the established firm than to the new entrant. Further, the existence of patents or other intellectual property in the hands of the established firm may give it better, non-public information about its costs.

A similar criticism of the McGee/Easterbrook view was recently presented by Schwarz, an official of the EC Commission[19]. Schwarz doubts that the McGee/Easterbrook model corresponds to real life situations, in particular to firms operating in multiple product markets. That is, given multiple products, the ability of a competitor to divine the predator's true cost structure is diminished, and the irrationality of predation less clear.

Although Schwarz writes in terms of the possibility of hidden cross-subsidization by the multiproduct firm, it does not appear that such cross-subsidization is necessary. It would seem that the competitor's information about the predator's costs could become equally confused whenever it was *possible* that the predator enjoyed some economies of scope, whether or not those economies actually existed.

Assuming, however, that the entrant and the established firm both have equal information, predation could still occur. Kreps and Wilson provide a model where both monopolist and entrant are equally uncertain of each others costs. In this model both the "strong" monopolist (i.e. low cost) and "weak" monopolist fight entry — the weaker firm because it realises that once it gives in in a market, entry can occur in all markets, as its reputation is then shattered. Assuming that the entrant has an equal interest in creating or maintaining a reputation, the entrant will seek to enter nonetheless[20].

The Kreps-Wilson and Milgrom-Roberts models have been criticised as unrealistic by one antitrust official. James Miller while Chairman of the United States Federal Trade Commission complained that:

> "These models also have some problems, however. Roughly speaking, they rely on a group of victims remaining passive while a potential predator invests in a reputation for toughness, after which the victims are convinced that the predator's threats are real. The problem with this logic, it seems to me, is similar to the problems with the old 'leader-follower' oligopoly models. That is, both models assume some firms will be content to be followers — or victims — despite the higher profits associated with a more aggressive strategy. Frankly, I don't find such a conceptualization of the predatory pricing story very descriptive of the tough [people who] run most companies!"[21]

These models, however, argue that potential entrants do not *know* the predator's costs and thus whether higher profits would follow from entry — if they knew the predator's costs, these models would be like Selten's and the threats would unravel. Their novelty is that they show what results when entrants are not sure whether the dominant firm is predating or has an unbeatable cost advantage[22].

A more telling criticism was later raised in a paper by Easly, Masson and Reynolds, who found the strategies available to the firms under the Kreps-Wilson and Milgrom-Roberts models too limited[23]. They present instead a more complicated model which allows for multiple market entry to overcome the predator and predation to delay rather than to eliminate entry. They find that despite these complications, predation is still a rational strategy to eliminate a rival, but can also be applied in other ways as well. They show that it could also pay to predate either "in perpetuity" in some markets to protect others or temporarily to delay entry[24].

The discussion so far has focused on whether or not it can ever be rational for a firm to engage in predatory pricing, ignoring the possibility that firms may engage in it without regard to its potential for maximizing profits. For example, Stelzer has recently argued that corporate managers may operate their firms to suit their own ends rather than the goal of profit maximization, citing the activities of corporate raiders as proof that numerous firms do not always work in their shareholders' interests:

> "In short, predation may not maximize profits. But it may nevertheless be a rational, far from unthinkable policy for business managers seeking to maximize their own career opportunities."[25]

B. Non-price predation

The discussion so far has focused on predatory *pricing*. The economics of non-price predation, however, are different and therefore merit separate treatment. The various methods of non-price predation have lately been seen as conduct which raises rivals' costs, in contrast with predatory pricing, which lowers their incomes. If a predator can successfully impose cost increases on its rivals, it can profit immediately even if the rivals remain in business, as its margins will increase disproportionately if the general price level rises. Conversely, if prices remain constant the predator should gain market share as its rivals restrict output. Thus, there is no notion of the predator suffering losses or foregone profits in the present in the hope of significantly greater gains in the future. Note also that, while the theories of reputation-based predatory pricing are largely built on pay-offs in other markets, there is no a priori requirement that a predator be a multi-market or multi-product firm to find it worthwhile to seek to raise its rivals' costs. All firms, even local ones, would benefit if their rivals' costs go up disproportionately to their own. Finally, while it may be more likely that a dominant firm will find it more beneficial to engage in non-price predation than will a smaller one, as any costs it incurs in predating can be spread out over a larger output, it is not necessary that the firm be dominant, particularly where, as will be discussed below, the predator can engage others, e.g. government, in actions against rival firms.

While not a new concept, non-price predation is receiving increasing attention. Bork, for example, has argued that predation can occur through the abuse of government procedures, including sham litigation and the misuse of licensing and regulatory authorities[26]. He cites the many types of regulatory hurdles to entry in a market, including controls by licensing authorities, health and building inspectors and planning boards and notes that an established firm can at low cost impose larger costs on a potential entrant, which will loom larger still if the entrant's initial sales or profits would be small[27]. Calvani and Tritell apply similar reasoning to foreign potential entrants, arguing that domestic firms may use sham proceedings under import relief laws, e.g. an unwarranted claim of dumping, to engage in non-price predation against a foreign rival[28]. Waller takes this concern one step further, finding that misuse of import relief laws can lead to collusive industry-to-industry settlements which result in cartelisation rather than vigorous import competition[29].

It has been suggested that non-price predation is not necessarily limited to the abuse of

13

governmental processes; advertising and innovation might also be used. In each case there is the ability for a dominant firm to spread fixed costs over a larger output than its rivals, and thereby raise costs disproportionately for those rivals. The difficulty, of course, is identifying which advertising campaign or R & D programme is predatory rather than competitive. Willig and Ordover, in the context of product innovation, have proposed that the line be drawn against those new products which would not be undertaken but for their ability to eliminate rivals[30]. That is, would a new product be profitable, after accounting for R & D and other costs, on the assumption that competitors remained in the market? If so, the innovation would not be seen as predatory. On the other hand, if the profitability of the product depended on its ability to cause exit, predation would be found.

Perhaps the most extensive writings on non-price predation have been by Salop, who has produced numerous articles in recent years[31]. He and Scheffman demonstrate how the predator can raise its rivals' costs, and thus its own profits or market share, through advertising or R & D efforts, through the creation of product standards or government regulations, or through exclusionary practices such as group boycotts and vertical price squeezes[32]. With Krattenmaker, he presents a theory of how various exclusionary practices can be seen as means of gaining monopoly power by raising rivals' costs. They look at the purchase of "exclusionary rights" as action which affects rivals' input prices, and view inputs broadly to include, for example, the "input" of a sales network[33], and present a number of vertical methods by which rivals' input prices can be increased. For example, an investment by a manufacturer in an exclusive distribution network may leave sufficiently few independent dealers that competing manufacturers face market power at the distribution level, raising those manufacturers' costs of distribution. This occurs not simply because the supply of available dealers has been reduced — so too has the demand for dealer services — but because of changes in market structure. For example, the remaining independent dealers may be so few in number that they can collude against the other manufacturers, or perhaps the predator provides them with some direct incentive to collude. Another example would be where the predator has foreclosed supply of a necessary input, perhaps by gaining control of the supply of the input or at least of its lowest cost sources[34].

Some economists, however, have criticized treating these types of conduct under the heading "raising rivals' costs". Brennan, for example, has argued that to the extent raising rivals' costs relates to the acquisition of market power in an input market, it offers little that is new; conventional horizontal market analysis can be used to examine monopolization of an upstream market. Moreover, he warns that the theory may be misapplied because it focuses attention of the costs imposed upon rival firms. Much pro-competitive activity, e.g. the introduction of innovative new products, will impose costs on rival firms. Such costs should not readily come under attack. A second problem posed by Brennan is that the notion of raising rivals' costs may misdirect attention to the wrong market. Thus, a firm's dealings in an input market may have the effect of raising its rivals costs and lowering their market share, but attention should be directed to output in the upstream market. If output there has increased, the conduct should be seen as procompetitive[35]. Brennan concludes that "antitrust enforcement will have taken a giant step backward, though, if RRC (raising rivals' costs) brings back the days when efficient vertical integration, exclusive dealing or charging low prices put a firm at legal risk".[36]

14

C. Discussion

The preceding discussion shows that the economics of price predation differ considerably from those of non-price predation. It follows then that the market conditions conducive to each type of conduct vary also.

Non-price predation does not presuppose multiple markets or products or any particular quality of information available to firms. Further, some types of non-price predation such as sham litigation or other misuse of government authority do not require the predator to be a dominant firm. Before competition would be affected, however, two conditions must be present. The exclusionary conduct must significantly raise competitors' costs and the output market must be such that there are barriers to entry and expansion in the output market[37].

Even where these conditions exist, a very cautious approach to claims of non-price predation is appropriate. When a firm undertakes capital investment, research and development, advertising, or vertical intergration, it may raise its rivals' costs, but such efforts are likely to enhance efficiency. Therefore, increased attention by competition authorities to allegations of non-price predation may deter procompetitive activity. Indeed, determining those rare instances when such normally productive practices are inefficient may be beyond the scope of the legal process. These concerns do not apply, however, when a firm engages in non-price predation by abusing judicial or administrative procedures to impede competitors.

The conditions for non-price predation are thus somewhat different from those for predatory pricing. According to some of the theories which find that predatory pricing can be a rational strategy, the following conditions are necessary:

1. The predator operates in multiple markets or produces multiple products;
2. Information is such that the victim and potential entrants are not sure that predation is taking place; and
3. Entry conditions, including the threat of predation, are such in the protected markets to permit supracompetitive pricing.

Note, however, that the promise of gaining or keeping supracompetitive pricing in the protected markets may not be a necessary incentive to the predator. It is conceivable that a firm earning normal returns in multiple markets could fear that new entry would create excess capacity and below-normal returns (at least until exit occurred). A firm in such a situation might predate in the first market entered in an effort to dissuade the entrant from expanding into the other markets[38]. Finally, note that a firm may engage in non-price predation against a rival by accusing the rival of engaging in predatory pricing. Misuse of the legal process can be minimized by assuring that any rule against predatory pricing is narrowly drawn.

III. THE FREQUENCY OF PREDATORY PRICING

The frequency with which predatory pricing occurs is disputed, which is not surprising given the underlying disagreements over its very rationality set out in the last chapter. Unfortunately, the dispute over prevalence is largely theoretical, as little empirical research has been done, and much of what has been done can be criticised. The evidence largely consists of case studies of famous incidents of alleged predation (based on incomplete historical data), efforts to create predation in laboratory experiments and studies of the frequency with which predation is alleged in antitrust actions in court proceedings. In addition, some competition authorities find that they receive allegations of predatory pricing with some regularity, particularly in jurisdictions where private actions are not permitted. Although these complaints are frequently received, relatively few are found to involve predation.

A complicating factor is that, according to the theories discussed previously, price predation *should* be difficult to identify. Those who argue that it can be a rational strategy find it rational only when the victim is unsure that predation is occurring — if the predation were evident the bluff should fail, following Selten. Given this prerequisite, the probability of finding good data on the observed frequency of predatory pricing is not high. The frequency with which predation occurs in one country may be a poor indicator of its frequency elsewhere. The likelihood that a firm will attempt to predate should be influenced by the legal rules and market conditions under which it operates, both of which can vary significantly from country to country.

Several writers beginning with McGee have looked at the behaviour of classic monopolies to determine if predatory pricing was used. McGee's original work in 1958 studied the Standard Oil Trust in the United States[1]. He found then, and reaffirmed in a more recent paper, that Standard Oil used mergers rather than predatory pricing to acquire monopoly power at the turn of the century[2]. He has likewise reaffirmed his belief that "attempts at predation have been rare, and that successful attempts will be found to be still rarer"[3].

Later, Elzinga studied the Gunpowder Trust, which operated in the United States in the last half of the 19th century. Based on a review of the record of a 1911 Department of Justice case against the Trust, he concludes that predatory pricing may have occurred but that it was less frequent than supposed and some factors, such as new entry and re-entry by victims, seemed to argue against it. Elzinga goes on to point out the difficulties of an historical search for predation: looking to what people say happened yields a self-serving and conflicting record. Further, price data existed but cost data was poor[4].

Yamey, on the other hand, looked to the use of "fighting ships" by a steamship conference as a clear example of predatory pricing and cites other examples as well: the case of "fighting brands" by the Canadian match monopoly in the 1920s and 1930s[5].

Another historically-oriented piece is by Burns, which examines the tobacco trust in the United States between 1891 and 1906[6]. Burns tests McGee's concept that merger is a more efficient monopolisation technique than predation by trying to determine through an econometric model the effect of the American Tobacco Company's alleged predation on its costs to acquire (1) the direct victims of the predation and (2) other firms (through a reputation effect). Burns uses a model which values firms according to current earnings, adjusted for risk and the present value of future earnings growth. Burns notes that the conduct of the dominant firm can either raise or lower the resulting valuation figure which it must pay for a rival. A non-predatory acquisition will have the effect of raising the valuations of the remaining firms to be acquired, as the increasing concentration raises the profit prospects of those firms. A predatory campaign, however, should reduce the valuation by reducing present and future prospects. He finds that predatory price cutting lowered acquisition costs by considerably more than it cost American Tobacco, and concludes that the McGee view on the irrationality of predation must be re-evaluated. In particular, he states:

> "The results ... tend to substantiate classical accounts of below-cost pricing by the old American Tobacco Company. They indicate that predatory price cutting directly reduced its expenditures for some alleged victims and, more certainly, created a notorious reputation that intimidated other competitors into selling out cheaply. ...[I]t appears that the trust repeatedly preyed on rivals both to offset the escalation of acquisition costs from peaceful output restriction and to lower those costs toward distress asset values. The estimated savings are quite large as well. The average discount from reputation effects alone is 25 per cent [citation] and an additional discount averaging 56 per cent accrued from preying on the relatively smaller fine cut, snuff, and smoking tobacco firms [citation]. These rates signify reductions in acquisition costs that are much greater than the trust's operating losses during at least one of the price wars in the sample: American Tobacco lost approximately $200,000 in the 'active competition' for control of the fine cut branch that was described briefly in Section III; but this campaign saved an estimated $1.07 million in the subsequent purchase of the McAlpin and Spaulding & Merrick companies [citation]. The corresponding net savings of almost $900,000 likewise exceed the estimated prewar earnings of these firms by about 2:1. Hence the trust may have been fully compensated for its direct losses and foregone monopoly profits from the fine cut contest, especially when the enhancement of its aggressive reputation promised to yield additional savings in the future. Thus, now that a rational basis for such misconduct has been documented, there are good reasons for believing that the numerous allegations of predatory pricing by the tobacco trust were fundamentally true."[7]

Note that the conduct studied by Burns occurred before the implementation of merger control in the United States. To the extent that effective merger control exists in a jurisdiction today, the incentive to predate as part of an acquisition strategy is correspondingly reduced.

Researchers using laboratory experiments were not able to induce subjects to behave as predators. In that test, Issac and Smith attempted to create conditions they thought would be conducive to producing predation: a two-firm market with one firm having a substantial cost advantage, a deeper pocket and sunk costs[8]. Entry and re-entry barriers existed and in most of the experiments neither firm knew the other's cost structure or demand, although the "predator" had a headstart in learning the demand curve. The most common outcome was dominant firm pricing and higher still shared monopoly pricing, the latter being seen most frequently in a subset of experiments testing the effect of certain antitrust rules against predatory pricing[9]. The Issac and Smith experiment may be an interesting effort, but its applicability to real world behaviour is unclear, especially since the model was limited to single product, single market situations where the research on reputation effects previously discussed suggests that the payoff from predation is the least.

Salop and White recently published a study of private antitrust litigation in the United States, collecting data on all such cases filed in five major federal district court jurisdictions (Manhatten, Chicago, San Francisco, Kansas City and Atlanta)[10]. Predatory pricing was not the most common allegation — horizontal price fixing and refusals to deal being alleged more than twice as frequently, as Table 1 shows.

Table 1. **Illegal practices alleged in complaints**

	Primary allegations	Combined primary and secondary allegations
Horizontal price fixing	15.7%	21.3%
Vertical price fixing	3.5	10.3
Dealer termination	4.4	8.9
Refusal to deal	12.0	25.4
Predatory pricing	3.1	10.4
Asset or patent accumulation	2.5	5.6
Price discrimination	5.0	16.4
Vertical price discrimination	1.7	5.8
Tying or exclusive dealing	9.6	21.1
Merger or joint venture	2.6	5.8
Inducing government action	0.5	0.8
"Conspiracy"	3.0	5.9
"Restraint of trade"	4.3	10.0
"Monopoly" or "monopolisation"	3.7	8.8
Other	8.6	8.9
No information	25.2	13.4

Note: Percentages total more than 100 per cent because a complaint may have more than one allegation.
Source: Salop and White, supra note 10 at 1006.

Not surprisingly, the plaintiffs in predatory price suits were most often competitors (in 138 of 257 cases of alleged predation), followed by dealers (56 cases)[11]. Of particular interest is that there is a clear trend away from allegations of predatory pricing in recent years, as shown in Table 2.

Such data in the frequency of allegations of predation is interesting but of limited use in learning the underlying frequency of predatory conduct. Rather, the sharp drop off in predation cases filed after 1979 probably reflects the ascendancy of the Areeda-Turner rule in American courts, discussed later in this report, which makes predation cases difficult for plaintiffs to win. In fact, the overall win rate for plaintiffs alleging predation during 1973-1983 has been low, implying that few recent cases are succeeding. By one measure, set forth in Table 3, only 7.3 per cent of all allegations of predatory pricing in that period resulted in a favourable judgment for the plaintiff.

Table 2. **Frequency of alleged illegal practices[1], by year of filing**

	Horizontal price fixing	Vertical price fixing	Dealer termination	Refusal to deal	Predatory pricing	Price dis-crimination	Tying or exclusive dealing
1973 and before	24.4%	16.3%	9.1%	26.3%	12.4%	23.4%	29.2%
1974	25.7	13.6	12.1	28.0	9.8	18.7	26.6
1975	20.5	7.3	11.7	25.4	10.2	20.0	29.8
1976	28.6	8.5	7.7	21.4	10.7	14.1	19.2
1977	17.3	7.3	6.4	21.8	11.4	17.7	18.2
1978	18.9	15.8	10.0	34.7	11.6	14.7	18.9
1979	18.2	13.3	11.5	33.9	13.3	21.8	19.4
1980	17.2	4.5	8.2	26.1	9.7	43.4	15.7
1981	19.6	7.1	10.1	24.4	8.3	10.1	16.7
1982	23.1	8.3	4.6	15.7	7.4	9.2	12.0
1983	32.1	8.0	2.7	15.2	5.4	9.8	17.9
All cases	21.3	10.3	8.9	25.4	10.4	16.4	21.1

1. Combined primary and secondary allegations.
Note: Percentages total more than 100 per cent because a complaint may have more than one allegation.
Source: Salop and White, supra note 10 at 1042.

Table 3. **Settlements and judgments, by alleged illegal practice relationships**

	Broad definition of settlements[1]		Narrow definition of settlements[2]	
	Settlement as a % of terminated cases	% of judgments favourable to plaintiffs	Settlement as a % of terminated cases	% of judgments favourable to plaintiffs
Alleged illegal practice:[3]				
Horizontal price fixing	84.2	24.6	68.3	12.3
Vertical price fixing	88.5	19.0	72.5	8.0
Dealer termination	86.2	43.5	74.5	23.8
Refusal to deal	85.6	25.4	68.6	11.6
Predatory pricing	92.9	23.1	77.6	7.3
Price discrimination	88.9	34.4	73.0	14.1
Tying or exclusive dealing	87.7	28.9	72.2	12.7
All horizontal	88.5	23.8	72.2	9.8
All vertical	86.9	27.9	72.3	12.7
All cases	88.2	28.1	70.8	11.3

1. Includes dismissals in settlements.
2. Includes dismissals in judgments for defendants.
3. Combined primary and secondary allegations.
Source: Salop and White, supra note 10 at 1045.

From the discussion above it appears that reliable information on the relative frequency of predatory conduct does not exist; the available information is historical and anecdotal. Moreover, even the historians are in sharp disagreement over whether celebrated past cases did in fact involve predatory conduct. The lack of "sightings", however, does not necessarily mean that predation is therefore rare. The theories presented in the preceding chapter which argue that predation can be rational assume facts which will make predation hard to find.

That is, to avoid Selten's "chain store paradox", these theories assume that predation is difficult to distinguish from competitive pricing; to the extent that the predation is obvious it is less credible as a threat and should not occur. Under this view, predatory pricing should not be dismissed as a phenomenon that cannot exist in the real world. As it will appear in Chapter 6 below, competition officials appear to face cases of predatory pricing today, even if infrequently or coupled with additional exclusionary conduct (e.g. the *ECS/AKZO* matter in the European communities). More frequently, however, competition authorities are presented with claims of predatory pricing by the self-diagnosed victims, who are often suffering only from vigorous price competition. To separate these complaints from the occasional case of predation, there is a need to develop economically sound rules for assessing conduct claimed to be predatory.

IV.   THEORIES FOR ASSESSING PREDATORY PRICING

The academic debate over the rationality and thus the frequency of predation is reflected in a parallel debate over the form of the best legal rule to control it. Broadly speaking, those who believe that the threat of predation is inherently incredible and thus that attempts to predate will be rare find that the best medicine is no medicine at all, given that any proscription could have undesirable effects on legitimate competitive pricing. Those who believe that predation is a real possibility are correspondingly more willing to seek to curb it, and seek to formulate more or less intrusive rules against predatory pricing. In discussing these proposals we will follow the convention in the literature and call the mistaking of predation for competitive pricing a "false negative" and the mistaking of competitive pricing for predation "false positive". Both types of error pose serious if different problems for competition policy. To impose no rule against predatory pricing may pose risks of greater monopoly power through increased concentration or more disciplined collusion among existing firms. Rules which are overly inclusive can likewise hinder competition either by detering firms from pricing agressively or by exposing those who do to public or private enforcement actions to make them stop. [Recall the discussion of non-price predation in Chapter II. A rule subject to false positive errors could be a potent weapon for a non-price predator which wishes to entangle a vigorous but not predatory competitor in an investigation or litigation over its pricing, at a minimum imposing substantial costs on that firm[1] and possibly promoting a cartel-like settlement[2].] Thus, the risks of false positive or false negative errors should be of concern in evaluating the various rules for analysing predatory pricing that have been suggested in the literature.

A.   No rule

Bork, McGee and Easterbrook[3] argue that predatory pricing is so rare that it should not be a matter of concern for competition policy officials. If predation is rare, practically any rule runs the risk of generating false positive errors, and those errors would multiply with the restrictiveness of the rule. An important point in this argument is that because predation is unlikely to be successful, it is self-deterring and therefore government intervention is unneeded. Self-deterrence arises because if a firm (foolishly) attempts to predate, it inflicts losses on itself but ultimately gains no market power, as the victim calls its bluff and weathers the predatory campaign. At some point the predation ceases and the predator, having punished itself, refrains from further attempts. Other firms, foreseeing this result, simply refrain ab initio from predating.

If in fact the business world conforms to this model, there is no apparent reason to intervene. As Easterbrook points out:

"conduct that might be predatory always involves lower prices, greater output, innovation, or other features that usually increase consumers' welfare. Any attempt to administer a rule against predation entails a significant risk of condemning the outcome of hard competition. The costs of litigating predation cases are staggering; no more complex cases could be imagined. And although a given price reduction or addition to plant *could* be predatory, it almost certainly is not. Similarly, price fixing or territorial allocation *could* be beneficial, but they almost certainly are not. If there is any room in antitrust law for rules of per se legality, one should be created to encompass predatory conduct. The antitrust offense of predation should be forgotten"[4].

Another argument that has been put for a no-rule approach is based not on the relative frequency of predatory pricing but on the inability of courts or competition authorities to distinguish predatory from competitive prices. If predation cannot be reliably identified (the "false positive" error discussed above), action against predation can proscribe efficient pricing in individual cases and have undesirable effects generally.

B. Short-run cost-based rules

Areeda and Turner first proposed their influential cost-based rules in 1975[5] and slightly modified them in 1978[6]. Areeda modified them again in 1982[7] and yet again (with Hovencamp) in 1986[8]. These rules are distinguished by focusing on short-run pricing conduct (when plant is fixed) and by looking at those prices in relation to costs rather than the intent of the price-setter. It is apparent that Areeda and Turner draw some of their inspiration from the welfare implications of marginal cost pricing and actively promote this in the design of their rules. The rules also seek to restrain firms as little as possible, reflecting their authors' view that predation is a rare phenomenon[9] and that a significant danger to competition would be a rule which competitors could turn against a firm's competitive pricing[10]. Areeda and Turner focus on short-run rather than long-run efficiency, even though they recognize that "strategic" long-run considerations may be important to the predator[11], because they find evaluating long-run efficiency too speculative[12]. Further, their concern is with designing a rule which protects only firms which are at least as efficient as the alleged predator; they are explicit that maximum allocative efficiency is a goal of their rule[13]. They recognize that, at least in theory, their rule would permit limit pricing and the exclusion of some firms which could (again at least in theory) increase competition further, but find that those benefits are speculative against the concrete present benefits of the monopolist's lower price and higher output[14]. They further argue that the administrative difficulties of reviewing the monopolist's pricing would be great[15].

Areeda and Turner focus first on short-run marginal costs to determine which pricing should be considered predatory. They then turn to average variable costs as a more practical proxy for enforcement purposes, given that accounting records are unlikely to yield meaningful information on marginal costs[16]. These variable costs are those costs which can be changed in the relevant time period, i.e. the duration of the low pricing episode; the longer the episode, the more costs which become variable. Areeda and Hovencamp find that the relevant period, absent special circumstances, is the middle run and would include, inter alia, general overhead, use depreciation and advertising and promotional expenses. Further, where capacity is being added, the incremental cost of that new capacity should also be included[17].

Areeda and Turner presuppose that the firm has monopoly power in the target market -

without monopoly power there would be no ability to extract future profits. (This point was expanded upon by Areeda and Hovencamp in 1986 and is taken up in part H below.) They would also define as per se legal all prices which are profit maximizing or loss minimizing for the firm[18]. Per se legality would also apply to prices above full average cost, even though not profit maximizing in the short run. That is, they would not be concerned about limit pricing, arguing that such pricing results in lower prices and higher output than the profit maximizing price and that only less efficient potential entrants are kept out in any event[19].

With respect to prices below average cost, Areeda and Turner would find predatory only those prices which were also below marginal cost. That is, prices above marginal costs but below average cost would be legal[20].

Areeda and Turner then transpose this group of rules to an average variable cost test and, in the 1975 version of their rule, argue that prices at or above reasonably anticipated average variable costs should be per se legal and prices below that level per se illegal[21]. In addition to these basic rules, Areeda and Turner would bar the dominant firm from "meeting competition" if it meant bringing its price below average variable cost and would likewise bar promotional spending, especially promotions designed to meet a competitor's promotion or new entry, if those additional expenses brought average variable cost above price[22]. The meeting competition defence was elaborated in the later supplements. Areeda and Hoven-camp, for example, argue that it should be available even to a monopolist if the plaintiff's price itself was unlawful, but not if the plaintiff's price was lawful, e.g. a promotional price by a small firm. On the other hand, the meeting competition defence should not be available to justify an unlawful price by an oligopolist responding to another oligopolist's prices, as such prices could inadvertently destroy fringe firms[23].

Areeda and Turner later modified their per se rules in important aspects. In particular, for prices above average variable costs they replace the standard of per se legality with a presumption of legality[24]. In the 1982 and 1986 supplements to the 1978 text, pricing below average variable cost would likewise carry only a presumption of illegality[25]. In any event, prices above full cost remain per se legal[26].

What would rebut these presumptions of legality and illegality? Areeda and Turner are not completely clear on this but some points can be drawn from their texts. First is the fact that the cost measure is defined as *reasonably anticipated* average variable costs[27]. Thus, an alleged predator could show that changed cost or demand conditions caused price to fall below average variable cost. Another rebuttal (here to the presumption of legality) would arise when pricing was at or above average variable cost but "significantly" below marginal cost[28]. Further exceptions are the defences of meeting competition and promotional pricing. Areeda and Turner would permit a dominant multi-market or multi-product firm to apply these defences if the firm could show that in the particular market in question it was not dominant[29].

C. Long-term cost-based rules

Posner has argued that long-run marginal costs are a better test of predation than short-run costs because the predator, by pricing at short-run marginal cost, could eliminate an equally or more efficient competitor (more efficient in having lower long-run marginal costs) but who lacked the ability or will to sustain losses in the short run[30]. Because marginal costs are hard to determine, he would substitute average costs from the firm's balance sheet, resulting in a test which would look to full average cost based on the company's books[31].

To this test he would add certain prerequisites, an intent element and a defence. As prerequisites he would require the plaintiff to make an initial showing that the market was predisposed to effective predatory pricing. Among the indicia he lists are that the predator operates in multiple markets, the prey operates in fewer markets than the predator, the markets are concentrated, entry is slow, fringe firms are few, buyers are numerous and the product is homogeneous[32]. He would further require that the predator have intent to exclude, but how that would be shown is unclear, as Posner himself finds that an intent requirement can lead to an unevenly applied rule — sophisticated predators will create no damning documents but unsophisticated and aggressive firms (or their zealous employees) could be expected to do just that[33]. Posner further would permit a firm to defend on the basis of changes in supply or demand, thus in light of excess capacity (e.g. a shift in demand) the defendant firm could price at short run marginal cost and the exit from the market which would follow would be socially desirable[34].

D. Output expansion rules

Williamson has proposed a complex set of rules which would govern both permissible output of dominant firms responding to new entry and permissible pricing by all firms[35]. His cost-based pricing rules will be summarized below, after reviewing his proposal relating to output restrictions. He argues that pure cost-based rules such as the Areeda and Turner proposal fail to take into account that firms will adopt their conduct, including their investment in plant capacity, to the legal environment[36]. Thus, the dominant firm could be expected to invest in sufficient additional capacity so that it could produce at high output in response to entry without violating the applicable marginal cost or average variable cost rule[37]. Until entry occurs, the firm would restrict output and raise price, maximizing profits at that level of capacity[38].

Williamson argues that these effects can be avoided by a rule which prohibits the dominant firm from expanding output in response to entry for a period of 12-18 months[39]. This time period is suggested as sufficient to allow the entrant to gain experience and customers[40]. Williamson would overlay this output limitation with a concurrent requirement that price not fall below average variable costs. If it should, the dominant firm would have to *reduce* output to maintain price[41].

Williamson puts forth two broad justifications for his rule: efficiency is greater both before and after entry and the rule is simpler and more certain in its operation. In terms of efficiency, the rule is designed to induce the dominant firm to increase output and lower price in the pre-entry period to be better positioned to deter entry. This will result in better plant utilisation and lower average cost in the pre-entry period[42]. After entry occurs, Williamson's model produces the same output for each rule, but shows that output comes at lower average cost under an output restriction rule[43]. He argues that such a rule is more easily enforced than a purely cost-based rule as the permissible level of output should be readily calculated, although some complications do arise[44].

In addition to this basic rule against output expansion in response to entry, Williamson lists a series of cost-based pricing rules. The basic pricing rule is that prices should cover long run average costs[45]; pricing that does not recover full costs in the long run could force out an equally efficient rival. This basic rule applies generally, except that new entrants would be permitted to offer at promotional prices (or even free) non-durable consumer goods for a very brief period[46].

Williamson's cost-based proposals have been criticized, e.g. by McGee[47] and Areeda and Turner[48], but we will focus here on the response to his output limitation rule. McGee finds

26

considerable fault with the theory underlying the rule, in particular that limit pricing is a viable way to exclude entrants. McGee argues that limit pricing should not deter because, as discussed in Chapter 2 above, the threat to expand output on entry is not credible. In other words, the scenario which Williamson seeks to avoid (excess capacity pre-entry, output expansion on entry) should not occur because once entry does occur, the dominant firm should co-operate rather than fight[49]. McGee further points out that there are costs in holding excess capacity pre-entry which, assuming that entry is deterred, would continue indefinitely[50].

McGee's criticism parallels the debate set forth earlier on whether a predatory firm can make a threat which a new entrant will not challenge and prove empty. The recent work arguing that such threats could prove to be effective in the case of imperfect and asymmetric information[51] in turn suggests that Williamson's concern over output expansion may in fact be well-founded.

Areeda and Turner take a different tack. They likewise are sceptical of the dangers of limit pricing but for different reasons and less vehemently than McGee. They argue that the gains from profit maximizing in the present should be more attractive than speculative future gains from deterring entry[52]. To them, limit pricing would seem sensible only where the dominant firm had a long-term cost or product advantage or where the minimum efficient scale was large in relation to output[53]. They further challenge Williamson's claim of easier administration, doubting the simplicity of forecasting the future demand which would determine the dominant firm's permissible output[54].

Concerning Williamson's cost-based rules, there is one point in the debate which is of particular interest. Williamson's basic cost rule is average cost, and he justifies it on two grounds. First, it provides a better measure of efficient resource allocation when the ratio of variable to fixed costs varies across competitors, particularly due to the application of different technologies. He gives as examples the differences between large-scale and small-scale mining and intermodal competition between common carriers. His second point is that differences in the degree of vertical integration can cause spurious differences in variable costs across firms[55].

E. Rules governing price rises

Another effort to control long-term "strategic" predation was by Baumol[56], who, like Williamson, seeks to avoid complete reliance upon cost based tests. While Williamson focused on controlling output increases in response to entry, Baumol aims at price increases *after* "successful" predation, i.e., after the new entrant has been driven off. Baumol would require any price cut made in response to entry to continue for a considerable period of time after exit. (Five years is the period he suggests.)[57] In effect, Baumol's rule would prohibit the capture of monopoly profits and thus limit the incentives of the predator to incur losses or forego profits in the first instance. The rule would not prohibit price cutting in response to new entry but would simply force the firm to select a price that it could live with in the longer term. The rule thus would avoid the necessity for computing any cost figure, as it would be left to the firm to decide what price was sufficiently remunerative. A further advantage of the approach would be that a new firm equally efficient with the existing firm should be able to survive, as any price cut selected by the existing firm should permit full cost recovery.

Baumol would, however, permit the alleged predator some leeway to raise prices after exit, although such an increase would have to be justified, at least as to a rough approximation, by changes in costs or demand[58]. Areeda and Turner have criticized the workability of Baumol's proposal, especially the ability of reviewing authorities to ensure that a price cut remains in effect for the required period following exit. They suggest that a predator could succeed in reraising price, possibly in several stages, by claims of changed costs and demand that would be difficult to refute. They further note that changes in quality or even in models could be used to obfuscate price changes, again defeating the purpose of the rule. A separate problem is that, by making price increases difficult, the rule might also make innocent firms leery of cutting prices, for fear of losing their ability to raise them again later[59].

F. Industry-specific rules

Some writers have recently argued that the creation of universally applicable rules is a hopeless task but that rules can be crafted to take into account particular industries. Craswell and Fratrik have taken on the case of supermarket retailing[60], which has recently seen allegations of predation by conventional stores responding to new entry by "no frills" discounters.

Craswell and Fratrik argue that allegations of predation in grocery retailing should not concern competition policy officials because of demand and supply conditions in that industry. They note that, apart from rapidly growing markets, existing capacity (in the United States) seems sufficient[61]. Because efficient scale entry implies a large new store, new entry will create excess capacity[62] and price cutting by the existing firms(s), even below their average recoverable costs, due to the existence of some restart-up costs[63]. This is a competitive rather than predatory response which should continue until capacity adjusts. Thus the competitive response to new entry looks just like a predatory one, and imposing a cost-based rule against predation risks inhibiting the competitive solution to excess capacity[64].

The difficulty they see in drafting adequate cost-based rules in this industry stems in part from the speculative nature of some of the adjustments which would have to be made to determine whether a price was predatory. For example, a loss leader sale could be non-predatory even at a price below average variable cost (e.g., below the wholesale cost of the item) given the revenue generated through the sale of other items (spillover revenue). Computing this spillover revenue, however, poses obvious difficulties[65]. Similarly, making sales below average variable costs can be loss minimizing in light of the costs arising from shutting down and restarting in the future, but some of these start-up costs are again speculative[66]. Thus, it is difficult to know whether current pricing is predatory or loss minimizing.

Structural characteristics, however, should make grocery retailing an unlikely candidate for predation. For example, start-up costs are low, especially for no-frills stores. Consumer loyalty is less of a barrier to overcome (the loyalty is more to the brands than to the store). Further, sunk costs are lower than in other industries (e.g., the inventory can be disposed of, the building sub-leased)[67]. Given these characteristics, any attempt by a predator to raise prices after inducing exit is likely to induce new entry. Hence predation is less likely to be a profitable strategy in grocery retailing than in industries where entry is more difficult.

Craswell and Fratrik do not however argue that predation can never be a rational strategy - they recognize that imperfect information can make predation work and that monopoly profits are not even a necessary inducement[68] - but that structural factors described above make predation unlikely in grocery retailing and rules which adequately distinguished competitive from predatory pricing could be impossible to administer[69].

A similar but more general result is reached by Areeda and Turner, who give "local distribution" as one example of markets where what they call the "prerequisites of predation" are absent[70].

G. Rule-of-reason tests

In response to the original Areeda-Turner rule, Scherer proposed a wide-ranging inquiry into many factors surrounding the predator's conduct, including the predator's intent and the consequences of its conduct. Scherer's goal is long-run allocative efficiency, a goal, he argues, which a simple short-run cost-based test will miss[71].

Scherer gives examples of scenarios where the Areeda-Turner rule would not maximize welfare. One is where the predator expands output when entry is threatened, leaving insufficient residual demand for entry on an efficient scale. Assuming entry is deterred, prices can result which are inefficient (below marginal cost) yet do not violate cost based rules (simultaneously exceeding average cost)[72]. Scherer also predicts that cost-based formulas could result in passive behaviour by the dominant firm and chronic excess capacity. This would result from the dominant firm being required to constantly cut output in the face of new entry to keep prices above, e.g., average costs[73].

According to Scherer, long-run welfare can be maximized, depending on the circumstances, with the dominant firm's price either above or below marginal costs. To determine the welfare maximizing price, he would look at the relative efficiencies of the firms in the market, the minimum efficient scale, the monopolist's effect on the fringe firm, whether the monopolist later reduced output and whether the monopolist adds efficient scale plant. These would be examined in light of the circumstances of the case, including the intent of the dominant firm and the structural consequences of its actions[74].

Although Scherer's early proposal to adopt a rule-of-reason approach was quickly denounced as unworkable, recent articles appearing in Europe have argued anew in favour of such a broad-based inquiry. In a recent paper published by the EC Commission[75], Phlips reviews and rejects the no-rule proposals of McGee and Easterbrook, finding that incomplete information makes predation a real antitrust concern. He likewise rejects the Baumol and Williamson proposals as under-inclusive and likely to facilitate collusion. Finally, he rejects the Areeda-Turner approach as both under-inclusive and difficult to administer, arguing that average variable costs are not easily described in practice.

Having found fault with the various bright-line rules, Phlips proposes a rule-of-reason standard "to establish predation with all available evidence at hand". The goal of his inquiry would be to determine whether the conduct of the predator has changed what would have been a positive entry value under normal competition into a negative one. [A positive entry value is defined as the situation where discounted future profits exceeds fixed sunk entry costs. Where costs exceed profits, the entry value is negative[76]]. Phlips defines the normal competitive price as a non-collusive profit-maximizing oligopoly price (a "Nash equilibrium price"). He believes that firms in oligopoly markets know such prices, even before entry, and thus that it is feasible to make Nash equilibrium-based pricing a key factor. As he envisions his test:

> "the victim should be asked to show a) that its post entry equilibrium market share and the equilibrium price(s) are such, in this market, that its entry value was positive and b) that, at the predator's price, this value became negative. The alleged predator's defence would be to show that its post entry price, in the local market in which entry occurred, *is*

the non-co-operative equilibrium price in this market, in the absence of compensations in its other markets. Its best defence would be to show that its post entry price in the entrant's market does *not* imply immediate foregone profits that are compensated by larger profits in its other markets, now or in the future. (The defendant could show, for example, that the alleged victim or other producers of the same commodity entered successfully - simultaneously or subsequently - in its other markets and reduced its profits there)."[77]

Phlips is not alone in calling for a broad-based inquiry. Schwarz's article argues that costs for a single product cannot be assessed when a multi-product firm is involved. His inquiry would include prices, capacity, investment, R & D, product innovation, advertising and marketing[78]. Likewise, Stelzer has recently stated that the pricing and other tactics of firms with market power should be examined against evidence of "intent, market power and the entire pattern of conduct of that firm in the market"[79].

H. "Two-tier" rules

Another approach which explicitly incorporates aspects of several of the rules described above is the two-tier approach of Joskow and Klevorick[80], which seeks to limit the focus of anti-predation law enforcement to those markets where predation is a serious threat, and then to subject pricing conduct in that narrowed target to more searching inquiry.

The essence of their approach is that market structure determines whether predation is a workable strategy. When predation is alleged, the market structure question thus should be disposed of first, in a bifurcated procedure, before opening up an inquiry into the defendant's conduct. This "two-tier" approach would lead to the more speedy elimination of harassment suits by competitors, limiting their ability to use the competition laws for protectionist purposes (or, as discussed in Chapter 2 above, as a method of non-price predation[81] by raising rival's costs). For enforcement officials such an approach would reduce the frequency of "false positive" errors, that is, wrongly identifying hard competition as predation[82].

The initial screening they propose would consist of three components - short-run monopoly power, conditions of entry and something called the "dynamic effects of competitors and entrants". Short-run monopoly power would be measured by the predator's market share and the elasticity of demand for its product. "Conditions of entry" refers to the speed with which potential competition can become actual competition in the event of supracompetitive pricing. Among the factors to be considered here are capital requirements, consumer loyalties, learning curves, the sequence of entry (market-by-market or across-the-board) and the quality of information about the risks of entry. The final component looks at the dynamics of the market. Markets characterized by rapid growth or by decline are said to pose less concern than markets more in equilibrium. Predation should also be of less concern where innovation and technological progress tends to come from the dominant firm than from fringe firms. Finally, the presence of price swings in response to changes in supply or demand are said to signify a market where predation is less of a risk[83].

If the analysis of first-tier factors reveals a market where predation should not arise, Joskow and Klevorick would permit any and all price cuts; no pricing rule would apply[84]. In this respect they echo other writers such as Posner, who made appropriate market conditions prerequisite to the application of his rule. Areeda and Hovencamp also find that such a first-tier review could be useful to dismiss cases where the prerequisites of predation are "obviously absent", but worry that the first tier would itself be complicated in less clear-cut

30

situations[85]. Nonethless, they emphasize in their 1986 supplement that certain prerequisites should be found before pricing should be challenged as predatory, including a large market share for the alleged predator (suggesting 60 per cent as the presumed minimum), a victim which is a minor rather than substantial competitor and entry barriers[86].

The second tier of the Joskow-Klevorik rule would include a broad inquiry into pricing, essentially a rule-of-reason approach, in which intent would be a relevant though not necessary factor and would incorporate a number of cost-based tests. Prices below average variable costs would be deemed predatory absent special factors which would make a temporary shut-down even more costly than sales at loss-making prices. Prices between average variable costs and average costs would be presumed to be predatory; the firm could defend by proof that the industry was declining or that the scale of new entry depressed prices. However, if the excess capacity was created pre-entry by defendant, then the excess capacity defence would not be available. Prices which remained above total costs would be presumed legal unless a price cut in response to entry was reversed within two years without a cost- or demand-based reason[87].

I. Discussion

The presentation of the various proposals above can create the impression that economists will never agree on what rule, if any, should govern predatory pricing. In fact, the situation is not quite so bleak; it is possible to find considerable common ground among a number of proposals.

Perhaps the most important single source of agreement is the requirement that the predator have some real measure of market power before a predation rule should apply. This is implicit in Areeda and Turner's first proposal (they refer to the predator as being able to regain losses due to "very high" barriers to entry and as a firm with "monopoly power"). Posner explicitly would make proof of market power part of the plaintiff's case. Williamson too takes the dominant position of the predator as given. Each of the proponents of a rule-of-reason test also assumes dominance. Finally, there are the two-tier and industry-specific approaches, each of which is explicitly based on the need for the would-be predator to possess market power. In the two-tier approach, the search for market power begins (and possibly ends) the inquiry. The Craswell-Fratrick approach is similar, but applied to an entire industry. Thus, significant market power, however defined, is necessary.

Second, there is a clear tendancy, even among the "all factors" proponents, to include some sort of cost-based test with which to judge pricing. While there is dispute as to whether the focus should be short- or long-run cost, and full cost versus average variable cost, that dispute is perhaps narrower than it might seem. Areeda and Turner, the main proponents of a short-run average variable cost test, include a number of items in their definition of short-run average variable cost which tend to bring that cost measure closer to full cost. They would exclude from variable cost only: "(1) capital costs (interest on debt and opportunity cost of share capital) attributable to investment in land, plant and equipment, (2) property and other taxes unaffected by output and (3) depreciation on plant (the life of which is little affected by use)"[88]. Thus such expenses as advertising, R & D, management and clerical expenses and all other costs would be included[89].

Areeda and Turner's cost definitions go a long way toward reducing the differences between their proposal and some of the others, but difficult questions get left behind. In particular, there is the problem that, in some industries, short-run marginal cost pricing may in fact be desirable at least in some circumstances. A current example is the airline industry, where the cost to the airline of filling an empty seat approaches zero as flight time nears, and consumers and the airline are both better off if low-priced stand-by tickets are available without regard to the full or variable costs of the flight as a whole. Categorizing such pricing as predatory would seem to promote inefficiency.

Most rules also recognize that general economic conditions should play a role in the application of pricing rules. In particular there are the overall capacity condition of the industry and the predator. There is a general willingness to permit below full cost pricing when excess capacity is present, e.g. due to a declining industry or a drop in demand. This is necessary both for efficient use of existing plant and to create the necessary price signals for capacity to adjust.

Perhaps the most troublesome area is the question of what besides cost will be evaluated. Intent is the single most important non-cost factor and there is widespread recognition that it can be useful, but equally widespread recognition of its limitations. In particular, looking to expressions of intent seems to increase the risk of both false positives (the zealous employee problem) and false negatives (the well-counselled firm problem). On the other hand, few commentators seem willing to close the door to receiving evidence of the dominant firm's intent. Another question relates to the timing of the low pricing. Are brief periods of price cutting sufficient to establish predation? Should low pricing early in a product cycle be treated differently from similarly low pricing later on?

The proposal by Phlips, standing alone, seems to pose a whole new range of problems. This rule would make the legality of the dominant firm's pricing dependent upon its effect on the *entrant's* profitability. This focus would add significantly to the dominant firm's uncertainty and risk, while creating room for inefficient entrants to seek to create a price umbrella.

Finally, there are the arguments against any rule at all. The argument by Bork, McGee and Easterbrook is powerful if one accepts their underlying assumptions. There is also the argument that any rule against predatory pricing, no matter how carefully and narrowly drawn, is likely to do more harm than good. It is argued that any rule inevitably will incorrectly condemn some and deter other legitimate, competitive pricing, and that this negative effect will outweigh the benefits from condemning or deterring truly predatory pricing. Considering, however, the recent literature discussed above, predation that produces reputational benefits across product or geographic markets, possibly to lower the cost of acquisitions or more simply to drive out or discipline rivals, perhaps should not be dismissed out of hand. Thus, per se legality of all pricing conduct is perhaps best limited to certain clearly-defined market structures where predation is unlikely to occur.

Accepting the case for some rule to control predatory pricing, an analysis of market structure and the market power of the incumbent firm seems to be a useful starting point for assessing alleged predatory pricing. This analysis would serve to eliminate from further inquiry many situations where successful predation is unlikely to occur. For the relatively limited number of remaining cases, cost-based analysis obviously must play an important role but other factors relating to the firm's overall strategy should also be taken into account when judging whether, on balance, a pricing strategy can be considered to be monopolization or an abuse of dominant position.

V. LEGAL MECHANISMS TO CONTROL PREDATION

This Chapter presents a country-by-country description of the competition law provisions available in some Member countries to control predatory pricing, primarily provisions relating to monopolization and abuse of dominant position. In addition, provisions relating to price discrimination are identified, as price discrimination may well occur if a multi-market firm is seeking to protect some markets by predation elsewhere. In addition, relevant regulations and proposed legislation or regulations are summarized.

Australia

Predatory pricing in Australia is subject to Section 46 of the Trade Practices Act, which deals with misuse of market power, and may also be subject to the price discrimination provisions (Section 49) of that Act.

A firm which engages in predatory pricing in violation of sections 46 or 49 is liable to civil proceedings in the Federal Court of Australia. The proceedings may be initiated by either the Trade Practices Commission (for penalties or an injunction) or private parties (for an injunction or damages). However, private proceedings which rely on the extraterritorial operation of the Act require the Attorney-General's consent.

Section 46 of the Trade Practices Act prohibits a corporation that has a substantial degree of power in a market from taking advantage of that power for the purpose of eliminating or substantially damaging a competitor, preventing market entry, or deterring or preventing competitive conduct. Prior to its amendment in 1986, Section 46 had been of limited usefulness in controlling misuse of market power, principally because it applied only to monopolists or those with overwhelming market dominance. Even when applied to monopolists, it was extremely difficult to prove the requisite predatory purpose in the absence of express statements of intent from the principals of the large corporations concerned.

Amendments to Section 46 effective in June 1986 are designed to overcome these two problems. First, the jurisdictional threshold was lowered so that the section now applies to corporations which have a "substantial degree" of market power. Previously, the corporation must have been in a position substantially to control a market.

A new sub-section 46(3) provides a guide to the way in which market power is to be determined. It requires that consideration be given to the extent to which the conduct of a corporation is or is not constrained by competition on the part of other participants in the market, potential entrants to the market, or its suppliers or purchasers. The circumstances which give rise to an absence of competitive constraint upon a corporation are diverse. They are not confined to size or market share in relation to competitors, or to those matters

33

combined with technical knowledge, raw materials or capital. Other matters such as easier access to supplies or capital or government controls on the market are relevant if they bear upon the extent to which the corporation can act without being constrained by competition. Thus market power can be derived from statutory limitations on competition (for instance, through the creation of statutory monopolies or restrictions on market entry) in the same way as any other constraints on competition can affect the operation of the market.

To assist in overcoming the second problem of proving predatory purpose, new sub-section 46(7) makes it clear that a court can infer the requisite predatory purpose from the conduct of the corporation. While explicit statements of intent may establish the necessary purpose, direct evidence of that kind is not essential. A related amendment extends the provisions of section 84 to section 46. Section 84 deems the intention of a servant, agent or director of a corporation to be the intention of the corporation itself. This amendment to section 84, combined with the inclusion of sub-section 46(7), is designed to make it easier for litigants, particularly private litigants, to establish predatory purpose.

Section 46 is aimed at the misuse by a corporation of its market power, which may include predatory pricing and price discrimination, but is not intended to restrain legitimate competitive behaviour.

Australian competition policy officials note that Section 46 does not set some particular cost floor; the prohibition in the section may be satisfied notwithstanding that prices are not below marginal or average variable cost and do not generate losses. They believe, though, that where a corporation with the requisite market power is selling at below average variable cost, there may be grounds for inferring that it is taking advantage of its power for a proscribed purpose, assuming no contrary proof that the pricing was not aimed at destroying actual or potential competition. On the other hand, Australian officials believe that Section 46 does not prevent a firm from pricing its goods very competitively by reason, for example, of economies of scale or the acquisition of new efficient production facilities even though it enjoys a substantial degree of market power. Low pricing due to efficiency, would not, without more, be taking advantage of market power notwithstanding any effect of such pricing on competitors.

Section 49 of the Trade Practices Act prohibits a corporation from discriminating in price between purchasers of goods if the discrimination is of such magnitude or is of such a recurring or systematic character that it has, or is likely to have, the effect of substantially lessening competition in a market. Discrimination is not prohibited where it is either cost justified or designed to meet a competitor's price. Price discrimination cannot be authorised on public benefit grounds. The adverse effect on competition of the discrimination must occur in either of two markets, the primary market or the secondary market. The primary market is that in which the supplier and its competitors sell goods. The secondary market is that in which the purchaser and its competitors resell.

Consistent with the broad thrust of the Trade Practices Act, the primary objective of section 49 is the promotion of competition. However, section 49 has the additional objective of assisting the competitive position of small business, but not as an overriding objective. Indeed, discrimination may result in the elimination of a small business but it may not have the requisite substantial effect on competition in the market as a whole for it to be in contravention of section 49.

The effectiveness of section 49 in achieving these two objectives has been widely debated. With respect to the promotion of competition, it has been argued that the provisions have operated to limit price flexibility. After section 49 came into operation in February 1975, there was some evidence that suppliers levelled out their discounts and this tended to raise prices generally. The Swanson Committee (a committee set up to review the operation of the

34

Trade Practices Act) recommended in 1977 that section 49 should be repealed because the anticompetitive effect of such price inflexibility outweighed any assistance small business may have derived from the section. Likewise, the Trade Practices Consultative Committee (the Blunt Committee) in its Report on Small Business and the Trade Practices Act in 1979 also recommended the repeal of Section 49. The Committee noted that as price discrimination requires some degree of market power for it to effectively harm or eliminate competitors, such predatory pricing is but one manifestation of misuse of market power. Accordingly, the Committee recommended that it would be more appropriate, and of more assistance to small business, for price discrimination to be regulated instead under a strengthened section 46 (it was recommended that section 46 be strengthened mainly by lowering the threshold so that the predatory conduct of a wider class of powerful firms would be regulated).

After considering the recommendations of both the Swanson and Blunt Committees, the Government decided to retain section 49 in substantially unchanged form because of its important role in the regulation of anticompetitive conduct and its particular benefit to small business. However, the amendments in June 1986 to section 46, partly along the lines recommended by the Blunt Committee, will extend its potential application to predatory price discrimination.

Austria

The main provisions relating to predatory pricing in Austria are found in the Federal Act of 29th June 1977 as amended by the Act of 6th March 1980 on the improvement in local supply and competition conditions. This Act prohibits the sale of certain products at or below cost price, which is defined as the price paid by the buyer to the supplier after deduction of rebates and special discounts allowed by the supplier on the invoice.

On the basis of this Act and of other regulations adopted under it the prohibition applies to dairy, cereal and meat products as well as to beer, eggs, fresh meat and poultry. The aim of the prohibition is mainly to prevent enticing offers and also to allow transparency of cost prices. In this way, enterprises with buying power are prevented from obtaining prices which fall below actual cost prices to the disadvantage of small and medium-sized businesses.

At the present time, the question is being discussed among interested parties as to whether the prohibition of selling at or below cost price contained in the Local Supply Act should be extended to a larger number of products. Legislative measures designed to achieve this are expected to come forward after they have been approved by the enterprises involved. A special prohibition procedure is used to enforce the regulations adopted in this area for infringements of the prohibition on selling at or below cost. The Cartel Court of the Superior Land Court of Vienna is the competent court for supervising the enforcement of this procedure.

It should also be pointed out that the problem of predatory pricing will also be dealt with in the framework of the new cartel legislation in so far as it falls within the jurisdiction of the Federal Ministry of Justice.

Belgium

In Belgium predatory pricing is subject to Articles 22 et seq. of the law of 14th July 1971 on commercial practices (prohibiting sales at a loss) as well as Article 54 of that same law (prohibiting acts contrary to "honest business" to injure competitors).

Article 22 prohibits sales by retailers or wholesalers to final consumers (which can include business buying for their own consumption) any product below its invoice price plus overhead and a normal profit. Sales which earn only "exceptionally low" profits or less after all expenses expose the merchant to an injunction against further sales under Article 55 of the Act, and a bad faith violation of that injunction can bring penalties under Article 61 of BF 1 000 to 5 000.

There are a number of important exceptions to the prohibitions of Article 22 and others are currently being considered by the legislature. In particular, manufacturers are not subject to its provisions (they lack invoice prices) as do sellers of services. Sellers otherwise subject to the prohibition may also take advantages of exceptions under Articles 23-31 for liquidations, sales (of seasonal, out-of-fashion or soiled goods), perishables, fad items, damaged or obsolete goods and meeting competition. Under Article 22, the King of Belgium can fix the minimum profit margins. A current bill in Parliament would modify Articles 22 and 23 by refining the consideration of low profit margins (sales volume and speed of turnover would be taken into account) and by adding additional permissible reasons to sell below cost (in connection with the opening of a new store and, possibly, the introduction of a new product, although a Senate amendment would drop the latter provision). Proceedings for violations can be brought by an interested party, including the Minister of Economic Affairs and trade or consumer associations.

Official commentary on the provisions have been published by the Ministry of Economic Affairs[1]. According to this commentary, the meeting competition defence in Article 23(f) is intended to be quite narrow, applying only to products which were heavily discounted before the introduction of the 1971 law. In all other cases firms are expected to bring an action for an injunction rather than meet the objectionable price[2]. The commentary also points out that the reach of Article 54 is considerably broader than that of Article 22, manufacturers and service providers are also covered[3]. This latter Article is said to apply to efforts to gain control of a market by sales which sacrifice profits to suppress competitors[4].

Canada

Predatory pricing is controlled in Canada under both the civil and criminal provisions of the Competition Act. Section 34(1) of that Act provides that various types of price discrimination and unreasonably low pricing may be punishable by up to two years imprisonment. Section 34(1)(a) provides that penalty for secondary line price discrimination while Section 34(1)(b) applies to geographic price discrimination which may substantially lessen competition, eliminate a competitor or is designed to do so. Section 34(1)(c) prohibits unreasonably low prices, again requiring a tendency to substantially lessen competition, eliminate a competitor or a design to achieve either effect. Section 34(2) requires that these unreasonably low prices be a "policy" rather than an isolated occurrence, such as meeting a competitor's price.

Section 50 and 51 of the Competition Act, on abuse of dominant position, provide essentially that where a person or persons substantially control a market and engage in a practice of anticompetitive acts that has prevented or lessened competition substantially or is likely to do so, the Competition Tribunal, responsible for adjudicating civil matters, may prohibit the practice or impose any kind of remedial orders. Several practices which relate to predatory pricing are specifically mentioned under Section 50. One of these is "squeezing" by a vertically integrated supplier, of the margin available to an unintegrated supplier, of the margin available to an unintegrated customer who competes with the supplier, for the purpose of impeding or preventing the customer's entry into, or expansion in, a market. Another is the use of "fighting brands" introduced selectively on a temporary basis to discipline or eliminate a competitor. Finally, there is selling articles at a price lower than the acquisition cost for the purpose of disciplining or eliminating a competitor.

Denmark

The Danish Monopolies and Restrictive Practices Supervision Act of 1955 applies to control predatory pricing. The Act can be applied by the Monopolies Control Authority to firms which have a "substantial influence" on market conditions[5] and which may cause "unreasonable prices"[6]. The reasonableness of prices follows from an examination of business conditions and assumes "appropriate technical and commercial efficiency"[7]. While these provisions have not been applied to low pricing (apart from loss-leader cases), the MCA believes that it would have the power to act if an appropriate case arose. Enforcement tools include the issuance of orders to cease violations, including orders which specify permissible prices[8].

Finland

The Finnish Parliament passed the Act on Restrictive Business Practices in Spring 1988 and that Act came into effect 1st October 1988. Under this act promoting entry into markets and preventing abuse of dominant market position will have priority. Abuse of the market position will be the criterion for evaluating the harmful effects of restrictive practices. One way in which a firm may abuse its dominant market position is predatory pricing. A price may be predatory if it is considered to distort competition by being *either* too high or too low. In this case, the Competition Council can set a maximum or minimum price for not more than six months to a commodity produced or sold by such a firm. There are no fixed criteria according to which the predatory aspects of pricing can be judged. Rather, they must be assessed on a case-by-case basis. This assessment should include the impediments to competition which enable the dominant firms to behave in a predatory manner.

France

Although predatory pricing is not separately defined under French law, France can reach such conduct under three statutory schemes concerning reselling at a loss, price discrimination and abuse of dominant position. In addition, predatory pricing schemes can be attacked under provisions relating to restrictive agreements and under provisions prohibiting of economic dependence. Finally, low-pricing practices can be attacked as unfair competition in the case of "prix d'appel", which involves advertised specials sold in limited quantitees at low margins, or as false advertising.

Reselling goods at a loss is prohibited per se under Law 63-628 of 2nd July 1963, which requires sellers to price at a level which, at a minimum, covers the cost of the goods, taxes and transportation. This provision applies only to the sale of goods, not services, and only to the simple resale of goods; manufacturers and processors are not covered. Several exclusions exist in the law for the sale of perishables, seasonal goods and obsolete goods. Sellers can also reduce their prices below historical (invoice) cost when replacement goods have fallen in price. Finally, they can lower prices to meet fair competition. Sellers who violate this pricing floor are subject to prosecution without regard to their intent to eliminate a competitor or to their market power and can be punished by penalties of from FF 5 000 to 100 000. Recent amendments under the Ordonnance of 1st December 1986 have liberalised the restrictiveness of this law somewhat by lowering the cost threshold to be applied. For example, the cost to the reseller will be reduced by the rebates he receives.

Price discrimination which is not cost-justified had been prohibited in France under Article 37 of Law 73-1193 of 27th December 1973. Intent or market power was not taken into account; the prohibition was per se. The Ordinance of 1st December 1986 decriminalised price discrimination, making it a civil offence whereby the offending firm could be held liable for damages by the court. The prohibition applies to any manufacturer or distributor, large or small scale, which practices a commercial discrimination against an "economic partner", creating a competitive advantage or disadvantage.

Apart from the provisions described above, selling at a low price in France is illegal only insofar as it amounts to an anticompetitive practice: cartel conduct, abuse of dominant position or abuse of economic dependency. These prohibitions are set forth in the competition policy provisions against "artificially low" prices, beginning with Article 50 of the Ordonnance of 30th June 1945, recently recodified by Articles 7 and 8 of the Competition Ordonnance of 1986. It is these provisions rather than the price discrimination provisions of the preceding paragraph which would be applied by the government against predatory pricing.

Article 50 prohibited, inter alia, "artificial" price reductions by concerted action or by a firm holding a dominant position which have as an object or possible effect a restriction on competition. Articles 7 and 8 of the new ordonnance modify these prohibitions somewhat. Article 7, as before, prohibits concerted actions when they are designed for or may have the effect of curbing, restraining or distorting competition, in particular when such actions may artificially raise or lower prices. Article 8, however, which relates to firms in dominant positions, does not refer explicitly to high or low pricing. Rather, it prohibits generally the abuse of a dominant position. Several non-exclusive examples of abusive conduct are given, notably including discriminatory sales conditions. The new provision of abuse of economic dependence can also be applied to control certain predatory actions, in particular actions by manufacturers to discipline discounting distributors.

A victim of predatory pricing in France can proceed in several ways. In the case of sales at a loss, he can seek to institute a criminal action. In the case of price discrimination, he can seek damages in a civil action. Competition law violations (abuse of dominant position) can be the subject of a complaint to the Competition Council.

Germany

Predatory pricing is actionable under two German statutes, the Act against Restraints of Competition (ARC) and the Unfair Competition Act (UCA). The ARC does not single out predatory pricing as an illegal practice, but such conduct can be reached by the provisions of the ARC dealing with abuse of dominant position, in particular Sections 22(4), 26(2) and 37a(3).

Section 22(4) permits the Federal Cartel Office (FCO) to prohibit abuses of dominant position, which are defined to include actions which impair the competitive possibilities of other enterprises in the absence of facts justifying such behaviour. Section 26(2) prohibits dominant firms from unfairly hindering other firms or from treating firms differently without justification. Under Section 37a(3), the FCO may prohibit a firm with superior market power from engaging conduct which unfairly hinders such competitors and is likely to unfair competition permanently. This latter provision, added to the ARC in 1980, is believed to cover a wider range of firms than Sections 22(4) and 26(2), given that its operation requires the defendant firm to have superior market power rather than a dominant position.

The other statutory provisions available against predatory pricing are found in the UCA, Section 1 of which provides that a firm acting contra bonos mores may be enjoined and held liable for damages. Conduct contra bonos mores can be found under this section in pricing below cost/purchase price designed to eliminate or discipline a rival by acts other than superior economic performance.

Private plaintiffs can bring actions under the UCA for injunctions and damages. Likewise, under Article 35 of the ARC, predatory conduct violating Section 26(2) may be the subject of an action for damages by victims or for injunctive relief.

Ireland

The Irish Restrictive Practices Act 1972, as amended in 1987, permits orders by the Minister for Industry and Commerce, on his own initiative or following an inquiry by the Fair Trade Commission, which prohibit unfair practices or unfair methods of competition, including predatory pricing. The power of the Commission to define predatory pricing as an unfair method of competition follows from a list of unfair practices set forth in the Act, including acts which:

(c) have or are likely to have the effect of unjustly eliminating a competitor;

***

(e) secure or are likely to secure, unfairly or contrary to the common good, a substantial or complete control of the supply or distribution of goods or any class of goods or the provision of services or any class of services;

***

(i) without good reason exclude or are likely to exclude new entrants to any trade, industry or business;

(j) secure or are likely to secure unjustly the territorial division of markets between particular persons or classes of persons to the exclusion of others.

Penalties for violation of the Act or of any order made thereunder include, for summary conviction, a fine of up to £500 together with a continuing fine of £50 per day for each day the offence continues. On conviction on indictment the sums are £10 000 with £1 000 per day for each day the offence continues or up to two years imprisonment or both fines and imprisonment.

The Commission decided in 1972, after consideration of all the issues involved in the grocery trade, not to recommend a ban on below cost selling as such, but to recommend the prohibition of "the advertising of products at a price less than the net purchase price by a retailer in any medium outside his own premises". The ensuing Order was amended in 1978 and introduced the concept of "net invoice price" as the definition of cost, replacing the "net purchase price". Following a review of the operation of the Order in 1986, the Commission came to the conclusion that, for a number of reasons, including difficulties of enforcement, the prohibition on advertising below cost had not succeeded in its objectives. These were to discourage actual selling below cost, which was always regarded as an undesirable practice involving a distinct element of unfairness and on occasion presenting some of the features of predatory pricing, and to prevent the increase of concentration in the grocery sector. The Commission's recommendation was that selling of grocery goods below net invoice price be prohibited by Order, with no exceptions apart from products excluded from the scope of the Order. This was included in the Order made by the Minister in 1987, with the further exception of three specified "seasonal products" and goods whose date of minimum durability ("best before" date) had expired.

Japan

The Anti-monopoly Act of Japan has no particular provisions specifically designed to take action against predatory pricing. However, there are three possibilities of combating such conduct under the provisions concerning price discrimination, unjust low-priced sales, and private monopolization. Section 19 of that Act prohibits entrepreneurs from employing unfair business practices which include price discrimination and unjust low-priced sales. The term "unfair trade practices" is defined as any act coming under any one of the categories of restrictive practices stipulated under Section 2-9 which tends to impede fair competition and which is designated by the Fair Trade Commission (FTC) as such. The FTC's designation of these two practices is:

"Price discrimination. Unjustly supplying or accepting a commodity or service at prices which discriminate between regions or between customers";

"Unjust low-priced sales. Without proper justification, supplying a commodity or service continously at a price which is notably below cost incurred in that supply, or otherwise unjustly supplying a commodity or service at a low price, thereby tending to cause difficulties in the business activities of other entrepreneurs".

Faced with a great number of complaints made by small retailers about large retailer's low pricing, the FTC in November 1984 published an explanation of the purpose and content of the regulation. Its main points are as follows:

i) A major purpose of the regulation on unjustly low-priced sales is to maintain a fair and competitive market, but not to protect the inefficient entrepreneur;

ii) Preconditions to determine if the case is "unjust low-priced sales" or not are as follows:
  a) the price is below a purchase price (a net purchase price after the deduction of discounts, rebates, free samples, etc.),
  b) the sales are, to a certain extent, carried out "continuously", and
  c) the sales may "tend to cause difficulties in the business activities of other entrepreneurs".

iii) A low price below the purchase price may be justified on the occasion of clearance sales of easily perishable goods like fresh foods and seasonal commodities after a peak season has past. It may also be justifiable to set a price equivalent to a declining market price due to the law of supply and demand.

Section 3 of the Anti-monopoly Act prohibits private monopolization which is defined in the Act as, "business activities by which any entrepreneurs, individually or collectively, exclude or control the business activities of other entrepreneurs, thereby causing, contrary to the public interest, a substantial restraint of competition." Dumping, discriminatory pricing, exclusive dealing, or controlling of necessary resources for manufacturing or selling are the most frequent methods employed to effect "exclusion". Exclusive dealing, resale price maintenance, tie-in contracts, mergers, stockholding or interlocking directorates are the methods usually employed to effect "control".

New Zealand

In New Zealand predatory pricing comes within the general prohibition on the use of market dominance for anticompetitive purposes contained in Section 36 of the Commerce Act 1986, which applies only to firms having a dominant position in a market. In the absence of market dominance there is no sanction or inhibition in New Zealand competition law against price cutting behaviour or price discrimination by firms not acting in collusion with others.

Market dominance in New Zealand is determined by examining:

"*a)* The share of the market, the technical knowledge, the access to materials or capital of that person or that person together with any interconnected body corporate;

b) The extent to which that person is constrained by the conduct of competitors or potential competitors in that market;

c) The extent to which that person is constrained by the conduct of suppliers or acquirers of goods or services in that market."

Section 36 prohibits market dominant firms from using their position of dominance to restrict entry, prevent or deter competitive conduct or eliminate any competitor.

Predatory pricing could meet any of these criteria. The test is related to purpose, rather than effect and that to come within the prohibition, the behaviour of the market dominant firm must involve the use of its dominance. The predatory conduct may be directed against participants or potential entrants into the market in which the firm is dominant, or participants in any other market.

Actions against violations of Section 36 of the Commerce Act are brought in the High Court by the Commerce Commission or by private litigants. The High Court may, when hearing such cases, be supplemented by lay members appointed for their expertise in industry, commerce, economics, law or accountancy. Remedies which the Court has available to it are injunctions, penalties of up to $300 000 (for cases brought by the Commerce Commission) and damages (for actions brought by private litigants).

Norway

Paragraph 24,1a of the Norwegian Act on Control of Prices, Profits and Restraints of Competition provides the Government's Price Directorate with two direct means to control predatory pricing. First, it empowers the Government to set minimum prices, effectively ending a predatory campaign. Second, in the event a predator were to succeed in gaining market power, that paragraph also permits the government to set maximum prices, thereby eliminating monopoly profits.

Portugal

Portugese competition law (Law No. 422/83 of 3rd December 1983) provides for the control of predatory pricing. Article 14 of this law prohibits the abuse of a dominant position with anticompetitive effects, including price discrimination. (Article 2 of this law defines a dominant position as one holding 30 per cent or more of the national market or not facing significant competition. In addition, there can be a "collective dominant position" in certain circumstances.) Article 13 of the law provides another mechanism to control predatory pricing involving a cartel, concerted action or the involvement of a trade association.

These provisions are enforced by the Director General for Competition and Prices, who must investigate following a complaint. Decisions on restrictive practices are made by the Competition Council and can be appealed to the Trial Court for Lisbon and then to the Court of Appeals.

Sweden

Sections 2 to 4 of the Swedish Competition Act, which deal with the elimination of harmful effects of restrictive business practices, can be applied to predatory pricing. In particular, the Market Court may issue an order against a firm causing, contrary to the public interest, "harmful effects" within Sweden, including effects which "unduly affect the formation of prices" or "impede or prevent the trade of others". Section 3 of the Act permits the Market Court to issue orders and injunctions against firms to terminate violations.

Switzerland

Swiss law contains provisions relating to predatory pricing under its Federal Law on Unfair Competition and the Law on Cartels and Similar Organizations. Under Article 3(f) of the unfair competition law of 19th December 1986, which took effect in Spring 1988, repeated offers through advertising of goods or services at prices below cost are considered unfair competition if such offers provide a deceptive picture of the seller's competitive position. Deception is presumed if prices are below cost but the seller has the possibility to rebut this presumption. A private party can enforce the provision by seeking an injunction or damages. In addition, intentional violations can be punished by imprisonment or a fine up to 100 000 francs.

Article 6 Section 2(c) of the Cartel Law of 20th December 1985 provides that selective price cutting designed to harm or eliminate a specific competitor is an illegal anticompetitive act, unless economically justified and not against the public interest. Affected parties can seek injunctions and damages.

United Kingdom

In the United Kingdom action may be taken by the competition authorities to deal with predatory behaviour under either the Fair Trading Act 1973, which provides for the investigation of "monopoly situations", or the Competition Act 1980, which provides supplementary procedures for the investigation of anticompetitive practices.

The Director General of Fair Trading has the discretionary power to initiate an investigation under either statute. Predatory behaviour can only be prohibited however if, after investigation, the Monopolies and Mergers Commission (MMC) conclude that the practice operates, or may be expected to operate, against the public interest and Ministers accept that conclusion.

In certain sectors of the economy action can be taken against predatory behaviour under other legislation. These are regulated sectors such as airlines and telecommunications.

The Competition Act is more likely to be used against predatory conduct than the Fair Trading Act, as it permits more focused and faster investigations. The Competition Act defines an anticompetitive practice as a course of conduct which has or is likely to have or is intended to have the effect of restricting, distorting or preventing competition in any market in the United Kingdom. Predatory pricing could be an anticompetitive practice under this definition. If the Director General does find it to be anticompetitive and the MMC, following a "competition reference", concurs and further finds it contrary to the public interest, the Secretary of State can use various order-making powers to remedy or prevent the adverse effects, or he can request the Director General to negotiate an undertaking. An order can in principle extend to structural relief; an undertaking will usually place conditions on future behaviour. Neither fines nor interim injunctive relief are available remedies.

The other possible method of proceeding is under the Fair Trading Act. This Act is applicable to a firm exploiting a "monopoly situation" (a market share of 25 per cent or more). Investigations are conducted by the MMC following a reference by the Director General of Fair Trading. The MMC determines whether the firm is acting to exploit or maintain its market power and, if so, whether those actions are against the public interest. If the MMC makes findings adverse to the firm, the remedial procedures described above come into play.

United States

In the United States, challenges to predatory pricing rest primarily on two federal statutes[9]. First, Section 2 of the Sherman Act[10] makes monopolization or attempts to monopolize any part of interstate commerce or commerce with foreign nations a felony, punishable by fines up to US$1 million for corporations, or US$100,000 for other persons. In addition, persons who violate the Sherman Act may be imprisoned for up to three years[11].

Second, Section 2(a) of the Clayton Act, as amended by the Robinson-Patman Act, proscribes price discrimination that may substantially lessen competition, or tend to create a monopoly, or "injure, destroy or prevent competition" with persons (or their customers) who grant or receive discriminatory prices[12]. In particular, primary line discrimination, that is, price discrimination that a firm employs to injure its rivals, may sometimes be considered a form of predation[13].

Private parties with standing to sue may seek enforcement under either the Sherman or Clayton Acts. If successful, plaintiffs can obtain injunctions, treble damages, court costs, and attorneys' fees[14]. A private plaintiff must make two allegations to establish its standing to sue under the antitrust laws: first, that it will suffer actual or threatened injury as a result of the violation, *Allen v. Wright*, 468 U.S. 737 (1984), and second, that the injury would be *antitrust injury*, *i.e.*, "injury of the type the antitrust laws were intended to prevent and that flows from that which makes defendants' acts unlawful." *Brunswick Corp. v. Pueblo Bowl-O-Mat, Inc.*, 429 U.S. 477, 489 (1977).

The Department of Justice and the Federal Trade Commission are responsible for governmental enforcement of the antitrust laws. The Department of Justice may seek injunctions, fines and criminal sanctions in court for violations of the Sherman or Clayton Acts. Through Section 5 of the Federal Trade Commission Act, which declares "unfair methods of competition" unlawful,[15] the Commission may seek injunctions or issue cease and desist orders for violations of the Sherman or Clayton Acts[16]. In addition, the Federal Trade Commission may challenge predatory pricing as a separate offence under Section 5, apart from the Sherman or Clayton Acts[17].

Monopolization in violation of Section 2 of the Sherman Act requires not only the possession of monopoly power, but improper conduct as well. As explained by the Supreme Court in *United States v. Grinnell Corp.*:

> The offence of [monopolization] under Section 2 of the Sherman Act has two elements: (1) the possession of monopoly power in the relevant market and (2) the wilful acquisition or maintenance of that power as distinguished from growth or development as a consequence of a superior product, business acumen, or historic accident[18].

Proof of the first element requires careful definitions of the relevant geographic and product markets, plus proof that the defendant does indeed have monopoly power within those markets, *i.e.*, "the power to control price or exclude competition."[19] It is well-settled, however, that the mere possession of monopoly power is not unlawful, because monopoly power may result from vigorously and successfully engaging in competitive activity that the antitrust laws are designed to promote. Thus, to proscribe the possession of monopoly power — or the exploitation of monopoly power by charging monopoly prices — would be unfair, and would also distort the incentives necessary for the competitive market to operate effectively[20].

The second element of the offence of monopolization focuses on the monopolist's conduct. Although "a monopolist is permitted, and indeed encouraged, by Section 2 to compete aggressively on the merits,"[21] it may not use its monopoly power to injure competition by excluding rivals unnecessarily[22]. In determining whether a firm has engaged in monopolizing behaviour, therefore, courts must look beyond the exclusionary effect on the victim — because this may arise from procompetitive or anticompetitive conduct — and consider the impact on competition and consumer welfare[23]. Where pricing or other strategies are intended to promote competition on the merits, courts generally find them lawful despite any exclusionary effect.

By contrast, an attempt to monopolize, which is also a violation of Section 2 of the Sherman Act, requires three basic elements: (1) exclusionary or anticompetitive conduct; (2) specific intent to control prices or destroy competition; and (3) a dangerous probability of success[24].

Like the conduct element for the offence of monopolization, the conduct element for the offence of attempted monopolization is essentially a test of the reasonableness of the challenged practice. As the US Court of Appeals for the Ninth Circuit has noted in comparing this aspect of the two offences:

> Conduct that does not constitute "wilful acquisition or maintenance" of monopoly power (thus precluding establishment of the offence of monopolization) *cannot* constitute the "predatory or anticompetitive conduct" required to establish the offence of attempt to monopolize.[25]

Generally, where conduct has a reasonable business justification (one that does not depend on successfully excluding competitors), courts will view the defendant's intent as competitive rather than as predatory. Thus, the Federal Trade Commission has held that "the legal and economic standard for evaluating allegedly predatory or discriminatory conduct should

44

carefully distinguish the structural conditions and behavioural patterns that are likely to improve competitive performance from those that are likely to injure competition."[26] The Commission offered three criteria to assist in such an assessment:

"(1) whether firms without substantial market power would find the conduct at issue to be profitable or economically rational; (2) whether the conduct improves product performance; and (3) whether industry conditions such as high entry barriers are likely to mitigate or accentuate any anticompetitive effects of the conduct. When properly defined, predatory pricing satisfies these criteria, because it is highly unlikely that firms without substantial market power will find it either profitable or otherwise economically rational; it is highly unlikely to improve product performance; and whether it will prove to be successful is largely a function of a variety of structural industry characteristics"[27].

In a similar vein, the Assistant Attorney General in charge of the Antitrust Division of the US Department of Justice recently stated:

"At a minimum, two basic and difficult-to-satisfy conditions are necessary, but not by themselves sufficient, for inefficient competition [such as predatory pricing] to be a rational practice: (1) the ability to inflict harm on a rival sufficient to enhance the predator's market power and (2) resulting ability to exercise the market power in such a way as to turn a net profit on the investment in predation."[28]

The specific intent element, sometimes described as the "specific intent to destroy competition or build a monopoly"[29], is an essential feature of the offence of attempted monopolization, but it need not be proven by direct evidence. Rather, it is often necessary to examine a defendant's conduct to determine whether otherwise ambiguous motives, such as the intent to drive competitors from the market, are predatory or competitive.

"Any successful business strategy will injure competitors to some degree; it satisfies the specific intent requirement only if it contemplates doing so by means of anticompetitive conduct. As the Commission recently stated, the specific intent element "is not satisfied by ambitious and aggressive plans to compete, even with the goal of taking business from competitors or vanquishing a troublesome rival. The antitrust laws provide no protection from such designs, where the means to effectuate them amount to no more than vigorous competition."[30]

Thus, a predator's improper subjective intent is often inferred from its conduct, particularly when that conduct would not appear to have a rational, non-predatory business justification[31].

Although some courts rely solely on conclusive or nearly conclusive presumptions of predatory or non-predatory intent drawn from objective evidence of a defendant's prices,[32] other courts urge reliance as well on other indications of subjective intent that may be available[33]. Courts express less concern, however, with the use of conclusive presumptions to create "zones of legality," which offer increased certainty to business managers, than with automatically condemning pricing conduct for which the record might reveal plausible, non-predatory justifications.

One of the federal antitrust enforcement authorities, too, has criticized the idea of relying solely upon numerical evidence in challenging pricing behaviour. The Assistant Attorney General in charge of the Antitrust Division of the US Department of Justice has observed:

"Unfortunately, the search for objective indicia that a practice is a form of inefficient competition [such as predatory pricing] seems ... fruitless. Asking whether prices are below some measure of cost — short-run marginal, long-run marginal, average variable or even, heaven help us, below the short-run profit maximizing price — may sound like neat, easy-to-apply tests, but they generally are not reliable. Uncertainty regarding which costs are relevant, what time period is significant, and even what the actual prices were, is likely to doom this inquiry to failure. Yet, even if a court is lucky enough to get the data to conclude positively that prices have indeed fallen below the relevant threshold for a substantial period, there often are legitimate and rational business reasons for selling goods below cost — indeed, even for giving them away."[34]

Finally, the offence of attempted monopolization in violation of Section 2 of the Sherman Act requires a "dangerous probability" that the effort will result in the acquisition of monopoly power. This element addresses whether the predator has the potential to succeed in its effort and may therefore seriously threaten consumer welfare. Traditionally, the starting point for this examination has been the predator's market share. In this regard, most courts seem to believe that a market share of less than 40 to 60 per cent, at the outset of a predatory campaign, is generally too small to create the requisite "dangerous probability of success."[35]

The FTC and the courts have made clear, however, that the assessment of "dangerous probability" does not focus solely, or even primarily, on the defendant's market share, but rather is multi-faceted. For example, the FTC has stated that the inquiry includes, among other factors, "the absolute and relative market shares [of the predator] and those of competing firms; the strength and capacity of current competitors; the potential for entry; the historic intensity of competition; and the impact of the legal or natural environment."[36]

In applying Section 2 of the Sherman Act to predatory pricing, courts attempt to assure that firms have sufficient latitude to compete vigorously and aggressively. The rationale for this approach is, as the Supreme Court recently noted, that "the mechanism by which a firm engages in predatory pricing — lowering prices — is the same mechanism by which a firm stimulates competition."[37] Since "cutting price in order to increase business often is the very essence of competition ... mistaken inferences ... are especially costly, because they chill the very conduct the antitrust laws are designed to protect."[38]

In addition to relying on Section 2 of the Sherman Act, public and private plaintiffs also challenge predatory pricing under Section 2(a) of the Clayton Act, as amended by the Robinson-Patman Act. The Act is quite technical in its requirements and interpretation. It prohibits "(1) a discrimination in price (2) between two buyers of the same seller (3) of commodities (4) of like grade and quality (5) where such discrimination may substantially injure competition in any line of commerce."[39] The Act expressly establishes specific defences if the discriminatory price is offered to meet the prices of competitors, reflects cost savings based on differences in the quantities of goods purchased or the methods of delivery used, or arises in special circumstances such as liquidation sales or the sale of perishable or obsolete goods[40].

One significant development over the past decade is that primary line price discrimination under the Robinson-Patman Act is being interpreted more harmoniously with predatory pricing under the Sherman Act. Traditionally, many courts viewed unlawful pricing — and particularly the concept of injury — differently under the Robinson-Patman and Sherman Acts. Whereas the offence of attempted monopolization under the Sherman Act requires proof of a dangerous probability that the price-cutting will result in monopoly, the Robinson-Patman Act requires proof only that the conduct "may substantially lessen competition."[41] One explanation asserted for this distinction has been that the Robinson-Patman Act was intended to protect competitors, whereas the Sherman Act is designed to protect competition. Under this view, which finds some support in the Act's legislative history, proof of injury to a competitor might be sufficient to support an allegation of price discrimination[42].

By contrast, the newer, and now prevailing, approach seeks to "reconcile the [Robinson-Patman] Act's protectionist undercurrent with antitrust's pro-competitive goals" by requiring plaintiffs alleging primary line price discrimination (*i.e.*, price discrimination involving injury to rival sellers) either to demonstrate competitive injury through direct market analysis, or to show injury to a competitor coupled with predatory intent[43]. Since neither injury to competition nor predatory intent is likely where pricing is above average variable cost, the Sherman Act's economically-oriented concepts of predatory pricing may readily be adapted for Robinson-Patman Act purposes[44]. This approach has been followed by Courts of Appeals in the Third, Fifth, Sixth, Eighth, Ninth, Tenth and Eleventh Circuits, and by the Federal Trade Commission[45].

EEC

Article 86 of the Treaty of Rome is the relevant provision in the EC concerning predatory pricing. Article 86 prohibits conduct which abuses a dominant position and which may affect trade between Member states. Article 86 sets forth four types of conduct which could constitute such an abuse, two of which could be applied against predatory pricing by a dominant firm. Article 86(a) prohibits "directly or indirectly imposing unfair purchase or selling prices or other unfair trading conditions", while Article 86(c) prohibits "applying dissimilar conditions to equivalent transactions with other trading parties, thereby placing them at a competitive disadvantage". These provisions are applicable to predatory pricing conduct in that low prices fall under Article 86(a)[46]. A firm making selective price cuts in one market or, alternatively, pricing low generally in one market to protect other markets, would run afoul of the price discrimination provisions of Article 86(c). Moreover, the prohibitions of Article 86 go beyond the types of abusive conduct listed therein; any conduct by a dominant firm which threatens the "structure of competition" in the Community may establish an abuse[47]. Note also that Article 85 of the Treaty, which controls restrictive agreements, could be applied to multifirm predatory conduct.

Actions may be brought directly by the EC Commission, either on its own initiative or on the application of a private party or a Member state[48], by a Member state in its own national courts[49], or by a private party in a national court[50]. Actions brought by the Commission can result in injunctions, including injunctions setting approved price levels[51], as well as penalties[52]. The remedies available to private plaintiffs in national courts is an evolving area[53] but it appears that both injunctions and damages will be available, at least in certain jurisdictions[54].

Discussion

This review of the laws of Member countries shows that there are numerous provisions available against pricing that could be considered predatory but no particular statutory scheme has been designed explicitly to combat such conduct. The closest approximation is found in the sale-at-a-loss provisions of Austrian, Belgian, French and Swiss laws. These statutes, however, are cast as unfair competition statutes rather than as statutes aimed at anticompetitive practices and thus do not require any type of market structure or market power analysis concerning the likelihood of anticompetitive effects of a predatory campaign.

The second group of laws relates to prohibitions of price discrimination which are found in Australia, Canada, France and the United States. These statutes can be of particular use in policing predatory pricing if the predator seeks to limit its losses by making selective price cuts directed towards its victim's customers but, as with the sale-at-a-loss provisions, not all of these statutes are based strictly in terms of economic efficiency. In addition, Article 86 of the Treaty of Rome applies to price discrimination likely to harm competition but the discriminating firm must have a dominant position and its discrimination must affect trade within the Community.

There remain those provisions aimed at protecting against monopolization or abuse of dominant position which exist in one form or another in most Member countries. These provisions are in general more rigorous in economic terms than the types of provisions described above, e.g. in requiring the predator to possess a dominant position in or a likelihood of successfully monopolizing a distinct market. On the other hand, these provisions, because they apply generally to monopolizing or abusive conduct, do not set out any particular test by which to measure pricing conduct. Thus courts and competition policy officials have some freedom in developing definitions of predatory pricing and therefore may be influenced by the various proposals by academics as to what conduct should be prohibited. One of the goals of the next chapter of this report, which examines case law in Member countries, is to see to what exent those proposals have shaped administrative policy and judicial precedent.

VI.   ENFORCEMENT ACTIONS

This chapter looks at how Member countries have applied their competition laws to cases including an allegation of predatory pricing. The examination of cases pays particular attention to the use of cost-related criteria by decision-makers and how they have categorized costs, e.g. between fixed and variable costs. In addition, the relative rigidity or flexibility of the various standards will be identified; does violation of a particular rule, e.g. pricing below average variable costs, create a per se violation or may a defendant defend the reasonableness of its pricing and by what proof? In addition to cost-based criteria, is it necessary to show predatory intent and by what circumstances may such intent be inferred? How have courts attempted to distinguish between aggressive competitive behaviour based on efficiency and abusive strategies aimed at reducing competition by forcing the exit of competitors? To what extent have competition authorities and courts considered the structure of a particular market when assessing the legality of a defendant's conduct? This chapter looks at these questions and then concludes with a brief synthesis which provides a comparative analysis of case law developments contrasting the main features emerging from the cases with the academic theories summarized in Chapter IV.

1.   Australia

A.   *Trade Practices Commission v. CSBP and Farmers Ltd* (1980)

This case involved a challenge under Section 46 of the Trade Practices Act alleging that pricing conduct by CSBP in response to new entry was a predatory misuse of market power. The case concerned the urea fertilizer market in Western Australia in 1975, a market which CSBP substantially controlled. The challenged conduct involved CSBP's response to new entry by Rural Traders Co-operative (WA) Ltd, which offered to import and supply urea at $145/tonne in face of a CSBP price of $178.70. CSBP responded by slightly beating the new price, offering urea at $144.60/tonne. Rural Traders withdrew in the face of this new price.

Although the Trade Practices Commission succeeded in establishing that CSBP was sufficiently dominant in the relevant market to fall under section 46 (and under the more rigorous standard which preceded the 1986 amendments), it did not persuade the Court to find the conduct predatory. The CSBP price reduction obviously injured the new entrant but the court would not find such conduct predatory without direct proof of intent to predate. The Court defined predation as:

> "conduct other than in accordance with the established practices of the company engaged in for the purpose and with the concern of damaging Rural Traders."

Note that the *CSBP* case might be decided differently under the 1986 amendments. Prior to being amended, it was extremely difficult under Section 46 to prove predatory intent in the absence of direct evidence such as express statements of intent by a principal of the corporation. The new sub-section 46(7) permits the court to infer an intent to abuse a dominant position from conduct and a related amendment makes a corporation responsible for the anticompetitive intent of its servants, agents and directors.

B. *Victorian Egg Marketing Board v. Parkwood Eggs Pty Ltd* (1978)

In this case, a number of the provisions in section 46 (again as it stood prior to its amendment in 1986) were considered without it being necessary for them to be decided, the proceedings being interlocutory. Nevertheless, the case is interesting in view of the consideration of one of the criteria for determining predatory pricing: the temporary nature of price-cutting activity.

Parkwood, an egg wholesaler in the Australian Capital Territory (ACT), supplied not less than 85 per cent of the ACT retail egg market. The Victorian Egg Board, a Victorian statutory corporation, wholesaled eggs for the Victorian retail market, where it had virtual control. As a statutory authority the Board was required to sell eggs in Victoria at a price reasonable to the consumer yet ensure a fair return to producers. It was not required to maximize profits and could sell surplus stocks at a loss. In short, its costs were unrelated to the costs of a private egg producer selling in the wholesale market. The Board's surplus of eggs not sold in Victoria were exported or sold interstate.

The proceedings in this case were precipitated by the Board's attempt to sell eggs in the ACT, offering eggs to two large retailers there at Parkwood's prices but subject to 10 cents per dozen discount for prompt payment. The two retailers together bought approximately one third of the eggs sold wholesale by Parkwood.

Parkwood sought an interlocutory judgment to restrain the Board, alleging that it was using its surplus eggs and the strength derived from its market position in Victoria to eliminate Parkwood from the ACT market. After a limited and urgent hearing, interlocutory injunctions were granted restraining the Board from selling eggs in the ACT at prices lower than those charged by Parkwood. The Board's appeal to the Full Federal Court was dismissed in August 1978. The Full Court considered that the Board was taking advantage of its power in relation to the Victorian market by engaging in price-cutting activities in the ACT, and that the Board's action had been for the purpose of deterring or preventing Parkwood from engaging in competitive conduct in the ACT market.

Parkwood alleged that the Board intended to sell in the ACT market at a price well below that charged in the Victorian market and such that Parkwood could not meet the price without loss. Nonetheless, the Board's prices were higher than those it obtained on its export sales, were not below its marginal or average variable costs and did not result in a loss being incurred.

The Board's pricing was still found to be predatory, however, given the temporary nature of the cuts and some evidence of an intent to damage Parkwood substantially. In this respect, the Court cited the view expressed in an American decision, *US v. Corn Products Refining Co*, 234 F 964 at 1012-13 (1916) that competition which is not intended to be permanent but is for a temporary purpose is a hallmark of a predatory practice and distinguishes it from legitimate competition.

2. Belgium

A. Sales at a loss

There have been a number of decisions by Belgian courts applying the prohibition of Article 22 against sales at a loss. A striking feature of these cases is that, as often as not, the plaintiff is the manufacturer using Article 22 as a means of curbing discounting and maintaining resale prices. Thus, in *S.A. Martini et Rossi v. P.V.B.A.R. et D.*, the court's calculations showed that the defendant had sold Martini without profit (but not at a loss) and ordered sales at that price to cease[1]. In *S.A. Brother International Belgium v. S.P.R.L. La Bureautique* the defendant was shown to have sold Brother typewriters for slightly less than their wholesale price in Belgium and with their serial numbers removed. The commercial tribunal of Mons ordered the cessation of both practices[2].

The provisions against sales at a loss have also been used by trade associations against discounters. In *Fédération nationale des négociants en bière et autres boissons v. S.A. Louis Delhaize*, a large retailer was challenged for selling cases of beer with a gross profit margin of approximately 5 per cent and net profits of about 1 per cent. The Court of Appeals of Brussels upheld a lower court decision finding that these margins did not constitute sales at a loss or at an exceptionally low margin in violation of Article 22. Notably, the Court of Appeals found that judges must consider the nature of the product and the form of distribution, along with other factors particular to each case, in assessing a firm's profit margins[3]. The same defendant faced an action by an association of bakery owners and certain individual grocers for bad faith sales of milk and bread at a loss. Finding both sales at a loss and bad faith (the store had been previously ordered not to sell butter at a loss), the court ordered payment of penalties and damages[4].

A number of these cases have made clear that the sale price must cover both a portion of overhead as well as the cost of the item[5], even for self-service stores[6]. This provision for overhead generally takes the form of adding a simple percentage figure to the invoice price[7], and one court has found that overhead must be spread across articles according to their sales volume rather than by the floor space they occupy[8]. In addition, there must be profit, as previously indicated, and this must be a net rather than gross profit. Further, special accounting procedures for sale periods are not permitted[9].

One exception to the general rule against sales at a loss appears however. Sales connected with the opening of a new store fall outside Article 22, as these are considered to be generally acceptable commercial practices[10].

B. Fegarbel v. Mobil Oil

Decisions by the Commercial Tribunal of Brussels and the Court of Appeals there in a recent case involving gasoline price wars further elaborate the sale at a loss prohibition of Article 22 as well as the prohibition against discriminatory pricing of Article 54. The case, *Fegarbel v. B.V. Mobil Oil and S.A. Seca*, was brought by an association of service station owners following a price war between Mobil and Seca in late 1983[11]. The trial court recognized that the sale at loss provision would not normally apply to a vertically integrated firm which sold directly to the public and that, particularly with multinationals, the costs to the firm were subject to manipulation and difficult to discern, a problem augmented by an oil glut and exchange-rate fluctuations. Nonetheless, Seca evidently admitted the violation and Mobil supplied figures which showed that its prices did not cover overhead and provide a profit, thus establishing a violation on its part. Both firms sought to invoke the "meeting competition" defence of article 23, which was rejected by both courts; Mobil as instigator of the discounting could not invoke the provision while Seca should have pursued Mobil in court rather than respond by cutting price, the price competition not being sufficiently widespread among competitors to justify invoking the exception (and Seca itself being partially to blame for the price war)[12].

The court's treatment of the charges of price discrimination under Article 54 is of particular interest as several facts about the case emerged, at least in general terms. First, Mobil, which initiated the discounting, had a distribution system composed of several distinct elements, including independent distributors and fully automated, limited service stations. Second, the discounting occurred in a depressed and declining retail distribution market. Third, Mobil had only a small (but unspecified) market share and faced powerful competitors. Finally, Mobil engaged in the price cutting as part of an attempt to increase its market share[13]. The trial court found that Mobil had not discriminated in violation of Article 54 even though its prices, reduced by from 20 to 58 per cent, were not sustainable in the long run and risked causing the elimination of a certain number of stations, because it gave equal treatment within each class of distributor[14].

The Court of Appeals reversed, finding Mobil guilty of a violation. Although the Court of Appeals affirmed the right of firms to price low notwithstanding the effects on competitors, it also found limits on that freedom where price discrimination was involved. These limits involved the means of discrimination, the depth of the discrimination and the effects. Finding that Mobil had in fact discriminated (but not describing how the trial court erred in this regard) and that the discrimination was the means to an illicit end (evidently an increase in its modest market share), the Court of Appeals found a violation of Article 54[15].

3. Canada

A. R. v. Producer's Dairy

A "policy" of predatory pricing was held in *R. v. Producer's Dairy Ltd.* to mean more than a short-term reaction to competition[16]. In 1961, one of the major dairies serving the Ottawa milk market offered a substantial price reduction to a supermarket chain in an effort to expand market share. This prompted Producer's to reduce its prices to retailers and to wholesalers. After two days, the low prices were withdrawn due to pressure by the union representing deliverymen, who had been adversely affected by the price war waged in the supermarkets. The charge of predatory pricing against Producer's was dismissed at trial and on appeal. While the Restrictive Trade Practices Commission (RTPC) felt that a policy existed due to evidence that Producer's had intended to broaden and continue their price offering, the courts viewed the low price as not being in the nature of a policy as it was withdrawn after two days, and hence was only a temporary expedient to meet aggressive competition. Further, because the price-cutting was a response to competitors, the court found that Producers lacked the necessary intent to discipline competitors.

B. R. v. Hoffman-La Roche

In the case of *R. v. Hoffman-La Roche*, which involved a free drug programme alleged to constitute predation, a major factor leading to the conviction was the establishment that this was "a planned and deliberate course of conduct by responsible employees of the company"[17]. As the result of changes in patent legislation, the large drug manufacturer and distributor found itself in competition with an entrant in the hospital segment of the tranquilizer market. In response, Hoffman-La Roche's strategy included large discounts on brand-name drugs, three one-dollar tenders to governments for supply contracts, and two six-month programmes supplying tranquilizers free of charge to hospitals and governments. The main issues examined by the Court were the reasonableness of price and the proof required to show predatory intent.

In *Hoffman-La Roche*, price-cost tests as the sole criterion were rejected as the word "unreasonably" in the statute suggested the need for flexibility and consideration of circumstances. Prices above cost cannot, it was held, be unreasonable. Unfortunately, it is unclear as to whether the "cost" referred to was meant to be average total or average variable cost. Prices lower than cost would not immediately be judged to be unreasonable even including a zero price, but would be subjected to further criteria such as the length of time the prices were in effect, the competitive circumstances of the sale, such as instances where price cutting is defensive in nature, and whether any legitimate long-term economic benefit such as market penetration or survival of hardship could accrue to the seller via below-cost pricing. Only the free drug supply programme was held to be at unreasonably low prices, considering the duration of the programme and the probability that legitimate future benefits would not compensate for the losses so sustained.

The court in Hoffman-La Roche found the requisite intent from several sources. First, it was inferred from internal corporate memoranda. Second, it was also inferred from the price cuts themselves given their magnitude, the losses thereby incurred and the lack of any other explanation for the price-cuts.

C. *R. v. Consumers Glass*

The issue of unreasonably low prices was paramount in the case of *R. v. Consumers Glass Co. Ltd. and Portion Packaging*[18]. Portion Packaging was the sole Canadian supplier of plastic drinking cup lids. In the face of declining sales volume, Portion had been maintaining utilization of plant capacity in order to offset overhead costs by pricing below average total cost, but still above average variable cost, for sales to the US, and planned to eventually leave the market. The entry of a large-scale competitor in 1975 sparked reciprocal price cuts through to 1979 involving losses for both firms. Subsequent price increases were not followed by Portion, which finally left the market.

Having found as a fact that Portion had priced above average variable cost at all times, the court adopted the Areeda-Turner standard and concluded that the prices charged were not unreasonable in the face of chronic excess capacity and with no evidence that the accused was not loss-minimizing. It is an open question as to whether a price between average total and average variable cost which was shown not to be loss-minimizing would be considered unreasonable. Some ambiguity also appears to exist regarding an appropriate test for "loss-minimization" and profit maximization.

Until this element is clarified, the position of the Director of Investigation and Research, as stated in his 1982 Annual Report, is that each situation must be examined in the light of relevant facts. Prices above average total cost would not likely be found unreasonable, and prices below this would be considered in view of their relation to costs, duration, apparent purpose, market position, history of the firms behaviour and apparent long-term consequences. Possible motives for predation and the amenability of the market to successful predation, i.e. whether entry barriers exist, will also be examined.

4. Denmark

A. *Ready-mixed concrete*

The Danish Monopolies Control Authority (MCA) has treated a single complaint of predatory pricing for ready-mixed concrete. It concerned a complaint from a Danish company, D.T. Beton Viborg A/S, that one of its competitors, Faerdigbeton Aalborg A/S, had in October 1985 set about selling certain qualities of ready-mixed concrete in the districts near Vejle at prices which were about 40 per cent below the list prices. According to the complainant, this initiative has only one purpose, namely to cut off D.T. Beton from the customers, and in doing so, to regain Faerdigbeton's own monopoly in that area and then raise prices again.

Faerdigbeton Aalbord A/S was notified to the register of the MCA pursuant to Section 6(2) of the Monopolies and Restrictive Practices Supervision Act, for production and sale of ready-mixed concrete. The origin of the case was at the beginning of September 1985. D.T. Beton had started a production and sale of ready-mixed concrete from a plant near Vejle, an area which had previously been controlled by Faerdigbeton. The MCA investigated to find out whether the prices charged by Faerdigbeton in the area concerned for ready-mixed concrete had involved a loss.

According to the available information, the calculated prices could be expected to cover the variable costs of the company, but only part of the capacity costs. Furthermore, the investigation showed that, irrespective of Faerdigbeton's price-cutting, D.T. Beton's sale of most concrete mixtures had been gradually increasing during the period 1st September 1985 - 1st November 1986, except that sales had as always been stagnant during the winter term.

On the present showing, the MCA found no proof that the price calculation in question had caused unreasonably low prices, and furthermore, it had been impossible to judge the extent to which the price calculation might have inflicted any adverse effects such as reduced sales on D.T. Beton.

Consequently, the MCA did not find sufficient reason to assume that the price calculation for ready-mixed concrete intended for sale in the Vejle area had caused unreasonable effects as mentioned in Section 11(1) of the Monopolies and Restrictive Practices Supervision Act, and accordingly, measures could not be taken in pursuance of Sections 11 and 12 of the Act. The MCA found, however, that the case gave rise to a more detailed investigation of Faerdigbeton's price calculations.

B. *Beer sales at cut prices*

In December 1984 Dansk Supermarked A/S and FDB submitted a complaint to the MCA, stating that De forenede Bryggerier had withheld supplies of beer in the period before Christmas from Bilka and OBS, because these discount stores had offered Hof and Tuborg beer for sale at just under Dkr. 100 a case, the purchase price being well over Dkr. 119. It was the opinion of the breweries that the refusal to supply was legitimate to prevent loss-leader sales.

As the discount stores could be expected to continue to sell below cost and the breweries would again withhold supplies, the matter was taken up for decision.

The MCA found that the law did not give the requisite authority to intervene by way of imposing orders to supply. The decision, affirmed by the Monopolies Appeal Tribunal, follows a policy that orders to supply, pursuant to Section 12(3) of the Monopolies and Restrictive Practices Supervision Act should be issued cautiously. Further, the fact that the goods were likely to be used as a loss leader justified the firm's refusal to supply. The decision provided, however, that the breweries' instructions to their store managers, which prescribed discontinuance of supplies when the dealers sold below cost, were consistently observed, so that all customers were treated equally. As it appeared that sale below cost was of very frequent occurrence - irrespective of these instructions - the MCA ordered the breweries, in pursuance of Section 12(2) of the Monopolies and Restrictive Practices Supervision Act, to revoke the instructions.

5. France

A. *Highway Drainage Castings*

In its opinion of 14th September 1978 in the matter of highway drainage castings[19], the Competition Commission examined whether the activities of Pont-à-Mousson S.A., which had become the industry's largest producer, abused a dominant position in violation of Article 59 of the Ordonnance of 30th June 1945. (Article 59 was later recodified as the Article 50 referred to in the preceding chapter.) Pont-à-Mousson had introduced in 1969 a superior line of products and began a series of investments in automated plant to increase its capacity. Further, thanks to productivity increases, its new line cost less to manufacture than its previous products.

The Commission found that Pont-à-Mousson had, beginning in 1969, established a goal of driving out its competitors and, in particular, of causing the failure of Queruel, one of its principal competitors. This was to be accomplished by selective price cuts directed to Queruel's customers, including some prices below cost, although cost is not defined in the decision.

The Commission's opinion noted that prices below cost do not necessarily violate Article 59; exceptions are made for firms seeking to penetrate a market or increase their market share. Violations occur, however, when below-cost prices are selective and offered with the intent of eliminating a particular competitor, especially when the predator is a dominant firm. Given that Pont-à-Mousson was dominant, priced discriminatorily and intended to eliminate a competitor, a violation of Article 59 was established.

B. *Charter Bus Service*

The Commission's view of abusive pricing was elaborated the next year in its opinion concerning charter bus service in Besançon[20]. That matter arose out of a private action, *Triponney v. Transgroup*, which in turn led to an investigation by the prosecutor and a referral to the Commission for an opinion.

Transgroup comprised a group of three charter bus companies (a "groupement d'intérêt économique") located in Besançon. Within the Department of Doubs, Transgroup provided much of the bus transportation, nearly 90 per cent of passenger service in the mid-1970s. Triponney, a school bus operator located outside Besançon, sought to enter the charter bus market and sharp price competition erupted between Triponney and Transgroup in 1974-75, including below-cost pricing by Transgroup.

The Competition Commission considered Transgroup as a cartel falling under the prohibition of Article 59 bis of the Ordonnance as it eliminated competition among the constituant firms. It declined, however, to find that Transgroup's pricing practices constituted a violation of Article 59 ter, as Transgroup's prices were in response to Triponney's own low prices and were not discriminatory. Because the pricing was not illicit, the Commission did not reach the question of whether Transgroup held a dominant position. The Commission explained that prices which meet or even slightly beat competing offers, provided that they are not discriminatory, do not violate Article 59 ter. The Commission viewed the situation as one of healthy and continuing competition rather than one of predation.

C. *Industrial Gases*

An opinion in the matter of industrial gases[21] followed shortly after the charter bus matter. This arose out of a complaint by a small industrial gas firm in southeastern France, la Liquéfaction de l'air, over the pricing and other practices of the Air Liquide group, which supplied from 61 to 100 per cent of various industrial gases in France in 1977, the figures varying according to the type of gas and the method of distribution.

The Commission's opinion examined the nature of the industrial gas market, finding an increasing concentration of suppliers due to changing technology (the use of liquid rather than compressed gas) and an insulation from interregional (to say nothing of international) competition given the cost of transportation. It thus concluded that Air Liquide had a dominant position on the French market despite the fact that foreign producers had recently expanded their market share.

The Commission found that the Air Liquide group had made cut-price offers to customers of la Liquéfaction de l'air after the latter had refused to enter into a market sharing and price-fixing agreement. The Commission concluded from the selective nature of the price cuts which had occurred in conjunction with other objectionable practices such as contractual provisions tying up customers for a long period of time that the pricing practices were intended to injure or eliminate the target firm as a rival. As there was sufficient evidence of predatory intent, the Commission did not feel it necessary to examine whether the prices charged by Air Liquide were actually below cost.

D. *Vinegar*

The question of "fighting brands" appeared in an opinion issued by the Commission later in 1979 concerning the practices of la Société Générale Alimentaire (SGA) in the French vinegar market[22]. The Commission found that vinegar constituted a fungible product which could be produced easily and with only a small investment. SGA, the nation's largest vinegar producer, held 36 per cent of the national market in 1978, down from 45 per cent in 1970-72 and produced a wide range of other food products. The next largest firm held a 7 per cent market share and evidently there were numerous small producers.

Among the activities of SGA which were reviewed by the Commission were those directed against a regional vinegar producer, la Compagnie française de condiments. SGA proposed that this latter firm reduce its production and limit its marketing to certain areas, in exchange for which it would terminate certain litigation against an employee of the firm. When la Compagnie française de condiments refused, SGA began a campaign of aggressive price competition, including sales below costs.

The Commission found that SGA held a dominant position in the vinegar market given its share of the overall market, its higher share (55 per cent) of the fine vinegar market with a well-known brand name and a broad product line. This position was abused by its aggressive below-cost pricing through a fighting brand whereas a high price level was maintained for its ordinary brand. The Commission then ordered SGA to cease offering similar vinegar under different names at very dissimilar prices in order to maintain high prices for one of its brands.

E. *Dipyridamole*

In 1983, the Commission issued an opinion concerning practices in the market for the drug dipyridamole[23]. Dipyridamole, a vasco-dilator used in treating heart ailments, is derived from another substance, DDH, which came off patent in 1976. The patent rights had been held by the German pharmaceutical group Boehringer-Ingleheim, which had several subsidiaries active in France, including Laboratoires du Sud-Ouest (Labso), Laboratories Boehringer-Ingleheim (LBI) and Laboratoires Français de Thérapeutique (LFT). Labso obtained DDH from its German affiliates and transformed that substance into dipyridamole, which it sold to LBI, which in turn packaged and marketed it under the name Persantine. Following the loss of patent protection in 1976, LFT began packaging and selling the same drug as a generic product under the name Peridamol.

The Commission's opinion focused mainly on the practices of these firms in the years following the termination of patent protection, when the firms acted to stem the loss of market share to new entrants in the production of dipyridamole. The group's share went from 100 per cent in 1976 to 81 per cent in 1981, and during that period the group engaged in several actions against its competitors, in particular a price war in the hospital market. In that market, LBI dropped its prices for Persantine in response to new competition to the point where it substantially undercut a competing firm, Bottu, going below its costs. This price war escalated through the use of free samples to the point where more product was given away than sold in 1981. On the other hand, LBI maintained a high price level for an identical product sold under the brand Peridamol to pharmacies. In addition, Bottu was at a particular disadvantage in this competition as it, like LBI, obtained at least some of its dipyridamole from Labso, an LBI affiliate. The Commission examined in detail the cost structure of the French subsidiary of LBI which it found artificially inflated by transfer prices for raw material supplies and by excessively high cost allocation for R & D. These high transfer prices helped to circumvent French price controls and, by moving profits upstream, put input-dependant competitors at a disadvantage. There was also evidence of other anticompetitive practices. The LBI affiliates also acted to try to keep other firms out of dipyridamole manufacturing. In 1977 and 1978 officials of the defendants warned two competitors of economic reprisals such as the breaking of a production contract if they did not withdraw from the dipyridamole market. Also threatened and put into place were efforts, ultimately unsuccessful, before the French health authorities to have competing products withdrawn from the market.

The Commission found that these activities, aimed at limiting the growth of competitors, abused the dominant position which the group held in the dipyridamole market. In addition, the Commission found that the sale of Persantine at very low prices in selective markets was used to maintain much higher prices for Peridamol in other markets. This practice and the Commission's handling of it were thus similar to the treatment of "fighting brands" in the vinegar matter discussed previously.

F. *Intravenous Solutions*

In the following year, the Commission examined practices in the market for intravenous solutions[24]. This market was shared by nine manufacturers, most of whom belonged to a trade association, Perfufrance, which set quality standards and performed research functions. Demand for the product came essentially from hospitals and, although aspects such as reliability were obviously important, the products were standardized and thus at least in theory subject to price competition. In practice, however, price competition generally did not occur as the firms divided up 97 per cent of the hospital market, a division enforced by fears that an attempt to move into a competitor's market would lead to a sharp counter-attack in one's own markets. Bid prices were known to competitors due to the practice by hospitals of informing firms of their competitors' offers. Further, the trade association provided a system of compensation between firms to correct "imbalances".

The only major challenge to the stability of this market-sharing arrangement came from several firms which were not members of Perfufrance. In one case in the period 1978-1980, a non-member firm Egic bid for a portion of the Lille hospital business. The three association members which bid in Lille responded by offering substantial price cuts on the products which Egic offered to supply but raised prices on the products not facing competition from Egic. (The Commission's opinion does not, however, indicate the relationship between the price cuts and the firms' costs.) In southwestern France, another new entrant was likewise hit with substantial price competition by association members, which lowered their prices by 30 per cent between 1978 and 1983 and gave away free samples as further rebates.

The Commission found these practices to be violations of Article 5O's prohibition against concerted action and fined three firms and the trade association over F. 2 400 000. Further, the trade association was enjoined from further actions facilitating concerted practices among the firms. As there was a clear violation of the anti-cartel provisions, there was no need for the Commission to examine whether the price cuts also constituted an abuse of a dominant position. Nor did the Commission consider it necessary to examine the relationships between the prices charged and the firms' cost.

G. Steel Reinforcing Bars

In 1985, the Commission again faced concerted practices in a concentrated industry, this time in the industry supplying welded steel reinforcing bars used in reinforced concrete construction[25]. This industry was dominated by the subsidiaries of two state-owned and subsidised steel firms, which held from 48 to 60 per cent of the French market between 1976 and 1984. Five domestic firms independent of the steel companies held from 15 to 20 per cent of the market during this time and imports from Belgium, Germany and Italy supplied the rest. Notably, the level of imports varied considerably with the prices charged by the domestic firms.

Unlike steel prices, the prices of welded reinforcing bars were not subject to price control in France and have fluctuated. Most price changes took the form of discounts from list prices and prices across the industry tended to be uniform at any one moment in time, reflecting in part the standardized nature of the product. Also contributing to this uniformity, however, were price-fixing and market-sharing agreements between the major domestic producers during the period 1981-84.

The Commission found that the price per ton of reinforcing bars dropped from F. 2 100 in January 1981 to F. 1 900 in April 1981, then rose to F. 3 075 in February 1982. By December 1982, however, prices had dropped to F. 1 600, only to reverse direction and climb again, reaching F. 2 800 by October 1983. Although the cost of steel rods, the major input, moved in the same direction as these price changes, the amplitude of the price changes were much greater than the changes in input prices.

The Commission's opinion sheds some light onto the causes and effects of these price changes. First, the rise in price running from mid-1981 to early 1982 was found to be due to a price-fixing and market-sharing agreement prepared by the leading French firm and accepted by a number of foreign and domestic firms. This led to prices in France substantially above those in the Netherlands, Germany, Switzerland and Italy. The high pricing, however, had several effects adverse to the cartel: buyers slowed their purchases and foreign and domestic firms not belonging to the cartel sharply undercut the cartel prices. Imports increased their market share from 16 per cent in April 1981 to 41 per cent in February 1982. These developments led the major domestic firms to begin a price-cutting campaign to regain their market share. By summer 1982, the import share dropped to about 20 per cent, but the dominant firms continued cutting their prices through 1982. The Commission found that the major firms thus took their prices below the cost of their steel input for some months in late 1982 and early 1983 and that the firms deliberately lost money in this period to regain their market share. Moreover, the Commission found that these firms thus intended to signal their competitors that they had the means through subsidies from their parent steel producers to discipline firms which would not obey cartel rules.

The predatory campaign did cause casualties, particularly among the independent domestic firms. One formerly profitable firm, Tréfileries du Sud-Est went into receivership, another dropped out of the market and a third survived but with a much reduced market share. This period of price-cutting terminated with another price-fixing and market-sharing agreement in September 1983, leading to the turnaround in prices described above. The Commission's opinion notes however, that the sharp rise in price in 1983 has been accompanied by an equally impressive rise in imports, with the import market share again reaching 40 per cent by June 1984.

The Commission found illegal concerted action causing artificial price increases and decreases. In addition, the Commission found a shared dominant position among the subsidiaries of the two domestic steel makers and that this dominant position was abused by the use of artificially low prices in 1982 to induce independent and foreign firms to join in a cartel. The Commission then imposed F. 6.5 million in fines against the four firms in the "shared dominant position" and an additional F. 600 000 against two trade associations.

Although the Commission's opinion as summarized above presents a seemingly straight-forward case of concerted price-fixing and market-allocation, the issue of abuse of a dominant position through the incriminated price strategies seems less clear. In particular, the opinion notes that contemporaneously with the price-cutting in France there existed serious overcapacity among German reinforcing bar manufacturers, leading to the approval of a temporary crisis cartel by the German Federal Cartel Office. Moreover, the German producers were considerably more productive than their French counterparts. The Commission found that the defendants could not justify their actions based on the German situation, but taking that point of view can lead to a different interpretation of events. In particular, by not viewing the French and German markets as sharply distinct (in fact, reinforcing bars were traded in both directions), one could find a larger market characterized by overcapacity and decline. In that situation price cutting, even below cost, could be seen as a desirable signal leading to reductions in excess capacity. Further, the ability of imports to respond to price increases in the French market suggests that the domestic producers might have been less dominant than it would otherwise appear.

6. Germany

A. *Benrath Filling Station*

Although it was decided prior to the enactment of German competition legislation, this decision handed down by the German Supreme Court (Reichsgericht) in 1931 is still valid today as a judicial precedent in distinguishing predatory pricing from competitive pricing behaviour[26].

At issue was a struggle between an independent filling station at Benrath and a group of major mineral oil firms both of whom initially charged identical petrol prices of 29 pfennig per litre at their filling stations. The group of firms then raised the petrol price to 32 pfennig, whereas the independent filling station continued to charge 29 pfennig. Having tried in vain to induce the independent dealer to raise his price to 32 pfennig, the group of firms lowered their price to 28 pfennig at their Benrath stations only. The independent dealer then reduced his price to 26 pfennig, whereupon the group of firms cut their price to 25 pfennig, and generally instructed their Benrath station owners always to undercut the independent dealer by 1 pfennig.

The Court considered the pricing behaviour of the oil companies as conduct contra bonos mores actionable under Act 1 of the Act against Unfair Competition and Article 826 of the Civil Code. In the Court's view the systematic undercutting of the plaintiff's price was designed solely to eliminate him through superior economic power as a competitor from the market. The objectionable conduct showing predatory intent was the fact that a particular competitor's price was systematically undercut without any consideration of cost nor any other economic justification. This was apparent from the defendants' instructions that their dealers should always undercut the rival's price by 1 pfennig. Moreover, the predatory nature of that strategy was highlighted by the fact that the rival had first been asked to raise his price at the same level as the group. Since the destructive purpose of the behaviour was obvious, the Court did not feel necessary to determine whether the price charged by the defendants was actually below cost.

In its opinion the Court made an important distinction which has remained a guiding principle for subsequent decisions. Competition based on economic performance is legitimate and each market participant is in principle free to sell its product at whatever price he chooses (Leistungswettbewerb). Competition through low pricing can only be considered unfair if, in the absence of other commercial reasons, it is designed for the sole purpose to eliminate or harm a particular rival and thus to restrain competition in the long run (Behinderungwettbewerb). Such intent can be inferred from conduct, for instance pressure on the rival to restrain its freedom to determine prices.

These principles have been confirmed in more recent decisions of the Federal Supreme Court (Bundesgerichtshof).

B. *Mineral Water Bottles*

In the context of occasional promotional campaigns the defendant, a supermarket chain, offered cases of mineral water for sale at prices clearly below its own purchase price[27].

In dismissing an action for injunctive relief by competitors the Court stated that the occasional sale of a product below cost (purchase price) does not constitute anticompetitive conduct if there are no additional elements of unfairness. Whether or not the repeated selling of a product below cost/purchase price is objectionable under competition law depends, among other things, on the intensity of such practices and the intervals between their occurrence.

C. *Electric Razors*

The plaintiff, a producer of electric razors sold under its brand name, attempted to prevent the resale below purchase price of this product by supermarket chains arguing that such pricing would prejudice the reputation of its brand[28].

In dismissing the action the Court held that selling below cost/purchase price is in principle not anticompetitive even where the sale of branded products is concerned. In the present market economy a merchant is free to determine its own price and this principle holds also for the relations between producer and distributors following the abolition of sale price maintenance schemes by the 1973 amendment to the Act against Restraints to Competition (ARC). Accordingly, the mere fact that a merchant suffers harm as a result of a rival's pricing does not, in the absence of other elements, suffice under competition law to constitute an act of unfairness.

D. *Abwehrblatt II*

In its decision of 10th December 1985 the Federal Supreme Court applied the above principles to the interpretation of Article 26 II of the ARC[29].

In this case the plaintiff, a producer of a local advertising gazette, brought an action for damages against the editor of a regional newspaper alleging that the defendant had as a defensive reaction established its own gazette offering below-cost rates of advertising. As a result the plaintiff was forced out of business.

After confirming the finding of the lower court that the defendant had market power in the relevant product and geographic market the Court drew the following distinction between predatory and competitive pricing.

-"... Undercutting a rival's price as such does not constitute unfair hindrance, but on the contrary is an essential element of competition. ..."

-"... Even where a market-dominating enterprise seeks to drive a rival out of business by its pricing, this does not as such necessarily justify a negative assessment. ..."

-"... In competition based on performance, hindrance that is justified must be endured. ..."

-"... In each particular case of undercutting, its target and purpose as well as the means used have to be examined. ..."

-"... Therefore, undercutting is considered unfair if it is aimed at a particular competitor with a view to eliminating and destroying him by means of unfair predatory pricing. ..."

However, the Federal Supreme Court did not decide the question whether undercutting a particular competitor's price to eliminate and destroy him by predatory pricing within the meaning of Section 26 (2) of the ARC was present in that particular case. The case was remitted to the appellate court for retrial.

7. Japan

Chubu Yomiuri Newspaper Co.

The Chubu Yomiuri Co., with the financial assistance of the Yomiuri Co., one of the three largest newspaper companies, sold a daily newspaper called the Chubu Yomiuri in three prefectures of central Japan at the monthly subscription rate of 500 Yen, which was substantially below its own costs of production and was much cheaper than other newspapers whose monthly subscription rates amount to 1 000 - 1 700 Yen. The FTC issued a complaint against the Chubu Yomiuri Co. alleging that such conduct by the respondent fell under item 5 of an FTC notification and violated Section 19 of the Act.

Before issuing the complaint on 25th March 1975, the FTC had applied to the Tokyo High Court for a provisional injunction, pending the FTC's decision, to stop the respondent's conduct temporarily because it was likely to cause irreparable damage to competition. On 30th April the Court accepted the FTC's application and held that the company must not sell its newspaper below cost, i.e. at a monthly rate lower than 812 Yen.

In the course of the formal hearing procedure, the respondent, accepting the findings as to fact and the point of law involved, requested a consent decision. Considering this appropriate, the FTC issued a decision on 24th December 1977, and ordered the respondent to sell the newspaper at a subscription rate of not less than 1 000 Yen per month.

8. Norway

Norcem Cement

In one matter involving Norcem Cement A/S the Norwegian Price Directorate used the threat of formal action to persuade Norway's only cement producer to stop what appeared to be predatory action. Faced with import competition in a local cement market, Norcem dropped its prices in that market alone. The Price Directorate, believing that Norcem was using its power as a monopolist to squeeze a competitor, advised the firm that it would require Norcem to price at that low level nation-wide. Norcem's response was to raise prices in that market, resulting in import competition.

9. Sweden

A. Svenska Shell

In 1975, the Competition Ombudsman investigated the pricing practices of AB Svenska Shell, responding to a complaint by a former Shell distributor, AB Karl Johannesson. Johannesson complained that Shell, after terminating his distributorship, began a price war in the sale of grade-one heating oil in his local market. The Ombudsman found that Shell's prices did not cover costs, taxes and charges and could, over time, eliminate local competitors. Although Shell claimed that Johannesson's prices were even lower than its own, it did agree to an undertaking with the Ombudsman. This undertaking commits Shell not to set prices in the Ljungby market which are significantly different from its prices nationwide. Further, Shell's prices must cover costs over the longer term, except for meeting competitor's prices or for other special circumstances.

B. Landstingens Inköpscentral

The Competition Ombudsman investigated similar practices in the market for health care products. Landstingens Inköpscentral (LIC), a firm which is owned by and does central purchasing on behalf of Swedish county councils, was the target of complaints by competing suppliers. LIC's business included the resale of these health care supplies not just to county councils, which purchase on a large scale, but also to municipalities, which are smaller customers.

The complaints, one of which sold disposable hospital supplies while the other sold veterinarian supplies, charged that LIC was pricing predatorily and the Competition Ombudsman's investigation bore this out. The Ombudsman found that LIC was pricing below cost in the municipality market and that these sales were subsidized by higher prices in the county council market, a price discrimination which could not be justified on a cost basis as the councils were the larger buyers. Some of LIC's challenged sales did not cover the purchase price of its goods while others did not cover that cost plus selling and handling expenses. Moreover, there was a danger of LIC achieving a monopoly situation if the practices continued, as one complaining firm was the only competition in the disposable goods market.

This matter was resolved by an undertaking by LIC to charge prices which covered its full costs plus a reasonable return. Further, its selling and other variable expenses would be apportioned by customer category according to the relative costs of supplying each category.

C. *Kronfagel*

On the other hand, the Competition Ombudsman investigated but did not challenge pricing practices by AB Kronfagel, the dominant chicken processing firm with between 65-70 per cent of Swedish production in 1987. Although the firm lost money in 1982 and had received capital funds from its owners (a farmers' co-operative), the Ombudsman found that market conditions rather than a predatory campaign were the source of low prices in the industry, pointing out that competitors' prices were even lower than Kronfagel's and that Kronfagel was reducing its capacity in light of the market situation.

D. *CPO v. National Telecommunications Administration*

In a private action in the Market Court, *CPO v. National Telecommunications Administration*, CPO charged that the NTA engaged in below-cost pricing in its sales and rentals of telephone answering machines. (In 1983, NTA had 50 per cent of this market, CPO 17 per cent and five other firms shared the remainder.) NTA's defence was that its pricing covered its variable costs and that it had no intent to eliminate CPO or other competitors.

In its decision, the Market Court looked to the legislative history and purpose of the Competition Act, which it took as preventing the abuse of market dominance. The Court indicated that its concern in this regard would be on harmful effects of low pricing rather than the pricing itself; pricing below cost did not necessarily offend the Act. The Court further stated that the NTA's practices merited particular concern in that NTA was not only dominant in the telephone answering machine market but also had a monopoly position in the supply of telephone services. The Court rejected NTA's defences concerning lack of intent holding that prices which could have harmful effects on competition were sufficent to make out a violation, regardless of the firm's intent. Moreover, the Court rejected NTA's defence that its prices were above variable costs, holding that fixed costs also had to be covered. The Court expressed concern over the possibility that NTA would cross-subsidize its non-monopoly business with profits from the monopoly side, restricting the long-term possibilities of competitors. Thus, NTA had to apportion its fixed costs among its monopoly and non-monopoly businesses. The inability of NTA's accounting system, however, to apportion these costs limited the Court's ability to resolve the issue. Ultimately, the Court decided that a change in NTA's marketing practices obviated the need for an order; NTA had essentially stopped renting its machines and the sale prices of its machines seemed amply to cover costs.

Note that the problems of cross-subsidization by national agencies brought out in the NTA case have been raised repeatedly in complaints to the Competition Ombudsman and by the Ombudsman before the Government. The Ombudsman has argued that the Post Office, the NTA and other agencies should account separately for their non-monopoly activities and that separate companies, where possible, were desirable. A bill passed in 1985 took up these concerns, requiring the Post Office to maintain separate accounts for operations in competitive sectors and to conduct those activities profitably.

10. United Kingdom

Over the years the UK competition authorities have had to consider a number of allegations of predatory pricing. Few of these have led to formal investigations under the competition legislation, although in some monopoly investigations by the MMC examples of predatory behaviour have been uncovered (a recent example in the concrete roofing tiles market is referred to below). Specific allegations of predatory behaviour will usually be examined under the provisions of the Competition Act 1980. The leading cases of this kind are referred to in the following paragraphs.

A. *Predatory pricing in the bus industry*

Since deregulation of the bus industry in 1985, the Office of Fair Trading has had numerous complaints of predatory pricing by incumbent operators of bus services. In two such cases, *Grey Green Coaches*[30] and *Eastern National Omnibus Company*[31], the Director General of Fair Trading decided not to initiate an investigation when the operators concerned amended the fares they had been charging (in the Grey Green Coaches case, a zero fare on its service to London from towns in Kent) and hence removed any ground for investigation. However in June 1988, the Director General did initiate investigations of alleged predatory pricing by two other operators, the *West Yorkshire Roadcar Company* and *South Yorkshire Transport*. These investigations were still in progress at the date of completion of this report.

Four other investigations under the Competition Act have been concerned with predatory behaviour.

B. *Scottish and Universal Newspapers Limited*

In a 1983 report under the Competition Act, the Director General of Fair Trading concluded that Scottish and Universal Newspapers Ltd. (SUNL) was pursuing an anticompetitive course of conduct which, due to the company's dominant position, had significant implications for the markets for newspapers and newspaper advertising in the Hamilton and Motherwell districts and adjacent areas of Scotland[32]. The Director General concluded that SUNL had taken steps which amounted to an anticompetitive practice and which could not be regarded as merely a competitive response to the setting up of a local rival free newspaper. The investigation found that SUNL had put pressure on the would-be printer of its prospective rival not to undertake the printing contract and had launched its own free newspaper within a week of the launch of its rival. It had then used this free newspaper to restrict the amount of advertising revenue available to a competitor, giving away large amounts of free advertising space over an unreasonable period and requiring exclusivity by advertisers. Further, much of the paid advertising was at a level below the marginal cost of its production and distribution.

The Director General concluded that SUNL pursued its course of conduct with the intention of frustrating the establishment of a competitor in the area in order to maintain in the long term the advertising rates, revenues and profitability of SUNL newspapers in the region. Matters of public interest were raised which were appropriate to refer to the MMC for further investigation. No reference was subsequently made, however, as SUNL gave to the Director General undertakings not to supply advertising space free of charge or at a charge which does not equal or exceed that part of the marginal cost of producing and distributing the paper attributable to that advertising space.

C. London Electricity Board

In 1982, the Director General of Fair Trading reported on the activities of the London Electricity Board (LEB) and found that the LEB had been pursuing a course of conduct which amounted to an anticompetitive practice appropriate for referral to the MMC[33]. LEB had been making losses in its business of retailing domestic electrical goods, spare parts and ancillary goods and these losses persisted at significant levels over a five-year period. The LEB's policy had been to charge prices similar to those of its competitors but which failed to reflect its own costs. In this way the LEB had maintained its market share at a level which would not have been possible for a private sector retailer unable to offset losses on the same scale against his other activities.

In their report in March 1983, the Monopolies and Mergers Commission confirmed the view that the LEB's management of retail sales involved an anticompetitive practice because there had been a persistent loss on the business, which had been financed out of profits from electricity supply where LEB had a monopoly[34]. The MMC concluded, however, that while the LEC's practice distorted competition it did not operate against the public interest because its effects were limited.

D. Customs Clearance at Welsh Ports

In a 1987 report, the Director General considered that Sealink Harbours Ltd had behaved anticompetitively in that its charges for customs clearance at two Welsh ports (Fishguard and Holyhead) were below the costs incurred by Sealink Harbours in providing the relevant services[35]. However, the report concluded that the effect on competition was unlikely to be significant since the difference between Sealink Harbours' charges and its costs was small, entry to the market was relatively easy and competitors were able to attract business even at higher charges than those of Sealink Harbours by offering a better quality of service. As a result no further action was taken in this case.

E. Becton Dickinson UK Limited

This report, published in June 1988, contains the most detailed analysis of predatory pricing so far under the Competition Act[36]. The investigation followed complaints that Becton Dickinson UK, part of a group owned by the American company Becton Dickinson & Company, had engaged in predatory pricing of the hypodermic syringes and needles that it supplied to the National Health Service.

The report commented that an assessment of whether a firm's prices are predatory should consider not only the relationship between prices and costs but also the structure and nature of the market for the product and any evidence of predatory intent. On the relationship between costs and prices, the report finds that Becton Dickinson's prices were not below its short-run marginal costs - the strictest standard for establishing predatory pricing. The Office of Fair Trading expresses the view in this report that prices may be predatory where they exceed marginal cost but are less than average total cost, depending upon the particular circumstances of the case. Although it had the largest market share, Becton Dickinson UK faces competition from several other significant suppliers, including other multinational companies. The analysis of the structure and other characteristics of the market suggested to the Office that there was little likelihood that a predatory pricing strategy by BD could be successful. The Office obtained no evidence of any predatory intent on Becton Dickinson UK's part and considered that its pricing policy was determined by the strength of competition in the market, stimulated by excess manufacturing capacity, the tendering procedures and the buying power of the various Health Authorities.

As mentioned above, over the years a number of monopoly investigations have established instances of predatory behaviour by dominant firms. In few cases has predatory behaviour been the main focus of the investigation, however, and rarely has the MMC's report recommended any remedial action. The most recent exception to this is the *Concrete Roofing Tiles* case.

F. *Marley Tile Company Limited and Redland Limited*

In 1981, the MMC reported on its investigation of the UK market for concrete roofing tiles[37]. The report concluded that as a result of the duopolistic structure of the market, competition had been restricted in some areas of Great Britain, resulting in higher prices overall than would have been the case in more competitive conditions. The MMC also found however that competition had been restricted in some areas of Great Britain, resulting in higher prices overall than would have been the case in more competitive conditions. The MMC also found, however, that in areas where they faced competition from small, local manufacturers both companies, in particular Redland, had given larger discounts than in areas where they held a local monopoly. The MMC were satisfied that Redland had not sold below average variable cost, at even its most heavily discounted prices, and accepted that its policy of competing on price, if necessary down to marginal cost, fell short of predatory pricing with the deliberate intention of eliminating a small competitor. However, they considered that both companies were able to contain new entrants' market penetration and accompanying price competition by means of selective discounting and saw Redland's behaviour as an indication of how deep selective discounting may be used by established firms as a means of preserving a dominant position. The MMC concluded that the adverse effects of the monopoly situation could best be reduced by the encouragement of increased competition from small manufacturers and recommended, inter alia, that to avoid new entrants or existing companies suffering from excessive discounting, the DGFT should monitor details of those projects for which the highest levels of discount were granted.

11. United States

In the United States, an extensive case law on predatory pricing has emerged since the passage of the Sherman Act in 1890[38]. Especially following the 1975 publication of a seminal article by Professors Areeda and Turner, the courts have mirrored the ferment in academia concerning predatory pricing, issuing probably more than 100 pertinent opinions. Until recently, this lower court activity also was fostered in part by the Supreme Court's silence on the issue[39]. In 1986, however, the Supreme Court decided two cases — *Cargill, Inc. v. Monfort of Colorado, Inc.*[40], and *Matsushita Electric Industrial Co., Ltd. v. Zenith Radio*

Corp.[41] — that reflect the emerging coalescence of academic and judicial views in the United States concerning predatory pricing.

The discussion following in Subsection A examines these two Supreme Court cases. Particularly because *Cargill* and *Matsushita* did not arise in the typical context of monopolization, attempted monopolization, or price discrimination allegations, the opinions leave many questions unanswered[42]. Subsection B, therefore, considers these issues in the course of reviewing seven significant Court of Appeals and Federal Trade Commission decisions.

A. *US Supreme Court Cases*

Matsushita Electric Industrial Co. v. Zenith Radio Corp.[43]

In *Matsushita*, a district court granted summary judgment in favour of 24 Japanese consumer electronics (primarily television) manufacturers. American manufacturers had alleged that the Japanese manufacturers conspired to charge supra-competitive prices in Japan in order to subsidize predatory pricing and other exclusionary activities in the United States. The Third Circuit reversed the grant of summary judgment with respect to 21 of the Japanese manufacturers. The US Supreme Court, in turn, reversed and remanded the court of appeals' decision.

Four attributes of the Supreme Court's opinion are important for purposes of this Report. First, the Court determined to examine separately the Japanese and United States aspects of the conspiracy. The Court reasoned that a conspiracy to charge supra-competitive prices in Japan did not have an impact on commerce in the United States and therefore was outside the reach of American antitrust laws. The Court also observed that a conspiracy to elevate prices generally benefits rivals, and therefore does not cause them the kind of antitrust injury required under the Sherman Act[44]. The significance of this analysis is that it rejects the kind of geographic cross-subsidization argument upon which so many predatory pricing and price discrimination arguments traditionally have been based[45].

Second, the Court applied economic reasoning to help assess whether the American manufacturers had presented a genuine issue of fact and therefore could survive a motion for summary judgment. The Court examined the American manufacturers' claims, both of conspiracy and injury, found them implausible from the standpoint of economics, and on that basis reversed the holding of the lower court[46].

Third, the Court examined predatory pricing from the standpoint of economic analysis, defining it "as either (i) pricing below the level necessary to sell their products, or (ii) pricing below some measure of cost."[47] The Court recognized that there are disagreements concerning the appropriate measure of cost, but it declined to address this controversy[48]. Similarly, the Court did not decide whether pricing above some measure of incremental cost could ever be unlawful[49]. Nonetheless, from a review of the academic literature, the Court concluded that "there is a consensus among commentators that predatory pricing schemes are rarely tried, and even more rarely successful."[50] Additionally, the majority recognized that difficulties of co-ordination, monitoring, and discipline make predatory pricing by a conspiracy far more complex, and therefore even more implausible, than predatory pricing by a single firm[51].

Fourth, underlying the Court's reasoning was special concern "lest a rule or precedent that authorizes a search for a particular type of undesirable pricing behavior end up by discouraging legitimate price competition."[52] This concern previously had been expressed in many court of appeals and Federal Trade Commission decisions[53].

Cargill, Inc. v. Monfort of Colorado, Inc.[54]

Monfort, the fifth largest beef packer in the United States, sought to enjoin an impending acquisition by Excel (the second largest beef packer) of Spencer Beef (the third largest beef packer). Even after the acquisition, Excel would have remained the second largest firm in the market, but would have more nearly rivalled the largest. Monfort contended that the acquisition would alter the market structure in a way that would subject Monfort to elevated costs, lower prices, and reduced profits. The district court held that this contention embodied a sufficient allegation of antitrust injury and granted the injunction. The court of appeals affirmed that decision. The Supreme Court, however, reversed the appellate court opinion and remanded the case.

In its opinion, the Supreme Court reasoned that business losses or reduced profits resulting from conduct that enhances legitimate competition does not constitute the kind of antitrust injury necessary to support a claim for damages. The Court also held that a private party should not be able to seek an injunction against conduct that would not justify an award of damages[55].

In assessing the substance and plausibility of Monfort's allegations, the Court initially considered the prospect that Excel might reduce prices to a level only slightly above costs. The Court reasoned that this pricing strategy would constitute a legitimate effort to gain market share, and found it "is in the interest of competition to permit dominant firms to engage in vigorous competition, including price competition."[56]

The Court then considered the possibility of below-cost pricing, and in the process elaborated on its *Matsushita* opinion in several significant ways. First, the *Cargill* definition of predatory pricing — "pricing below an appropriate measure of cost for the purpose of eliminating competitors in the short run and reducing competition in the long run"[57] — clearly allows for the possibility that some below cost pricing may be well-intended and lawful.

Second, the Court examined the economic prerequisites for a successful predatory pricing campaign. In this regard, it specifically recognized the importance of entry barriers and of the predator's capacity to absorb its victims' market shares[58]. Thus, the Court implicitly rejected reliance solely on price-cost comparisons.

Third, the Court reiterated its views, expressed in *Matsushita*, that predatory pricing is seldom rational and therefore rare[59]. The Court, however, also acknowledged that "[w]hile firms may engage in the practice only infrequently, there is ample evidence suggesting that the practice does occur."[60] Accordingly, the Court expressly rejected an argument advanced by the US Department of Justice and the Federal Trade Commission, as amici curiae, urging establishment of a rule that would have, in essence, precluded all challenges to acquisitions by competitors based on predatory pricing theories[61].

B. *Lower Federal Court Predatory Pricing Cases*

Although *Cargill* and *Matsushita* helped refine the judicial definition of predatory pricing, and provided guidance on how courts should address predatory pricing allegations, the decisions left other issues unaddressed. This section, therefore, examines seven recent or frequently-cited predatory pricing decisions of federal courts of appeals and the Federal Trade Commission[62]. The review is designed particularly to show the judicial foundations of the Supreme Court's reasoning in *Cargill* and *Matsushita*, to consider various lower court views on some as yet unresolved predatory pricing issues, and to spotlight some key legal, economic, and jurisprudential themes that are prominent in the analyses of the lower courts. These themes include:

a) Primary emphasis on the challenged pricing activity's impact on consumers and consumer welfare, rather than its impact on competitors;

b) Concern that overly-broad predatory pricing enforcement efforts may chill the vigorous price competition that the antitrust laws are intended to promote;

c) Use of increasingly sophisticated economic analysis to define product and geographic markets, allocate costs, and determine whether below-cost pricing would be a profitable anticompetitive strategy in a given market; and

d) Recognition that price-cost presumptions are useful in determining when pricing may injure consumer welfare and be motivated by predatory intent. The set of presumptions adopted by any given court reflect that court's concern with achieving maximum allocative efficiency; its views regarding the frequency of successful predation; its confidence that costs can be readily and reliably calculated and allocated; and its desire to consider other, non-cost factors (e.g., direct evidence of intent, market power, market structure, long-run effects).

At present, the majority approach entails the following presumptions:

1. Prices below average variable cost are rebuttably presumed unlawful;
2. Prices above average variable cost and below average total cost are rebuttably presumed lawful; and
3. Prices above average total cost are strongly, and in some jurisdictions conclusively, presumed lawful.

Three other important themes are omitted from this review because the issues are examined in Chapter V's discussion of United States law. These themes are that (1) predatory pricing analysis should be evaluated according to the same principles under both the Sherman and Robinson-Patman Acts; (2) analysis of an alleged predator's conduct often clarifies ambiguous evidence regarding its intent, and (3) in most circuits, proof that challenged conduct has a dangerous probability of success must rest on a foundational showing that the alleged predator has some market power.

Janich Bros. Inc. v. American Distilling Co.[63]

In *Janich*, the Ninth Circuit affirmed the trial court's determinations to dismiss (by directed verdict) the plaintiff's attempted monopolization claim and to reject a jury verdict that the defendant had engaged in price discrimination. Janich Bros., a firm that bottled and distributed alcoholic beverages in California, had charged that the defendant's prices on one-half gallon bottles of gin and vodka were predatory because they were below cost.

The court of appeals faulted plaintiff's case in three ways. First, plaintiff asserted that defendant's costs were its "cost of merchandise sold," as reflected in defendant's accounting records. This cost figure, which the defendant had computed to conform to Securities and Exchange Commission requirements, was higher than marginal or average variable cost figure because it included certain fixed costs[64]. Second, plaintiff incorrectly focused only on prices for half-gallon sizes, which did not constitute a separate product for purposes of analyzing predatory pricing. Rather, because liquor was wholesaled in several different sizes and most retailers took the whole line, plaintiff would have needed to show that the entire line was priced below average variable cost[65]. Third, plaintiff's evidence was insufficient to demonstrate that the defendant's conduct would have any detrimental impact on competition, as required by both the Sherman Act and Robinson-Patman Act. Each of these three issues — cost computation, market definition, and antitrust injury — have frequently posed major problems of proof for antitrust plaintiffs in predatory pricing cases.

In general, *Janich* adheres closely to the Areeda-Turner analysis. In particular, the court emphasized the commentators' efficiency-based rationale, agreed that long-run welfare effects were difficult to assess, and accepted that a marginal cost (or average variable cost) standard would be most useful for assessing short-run consumer welfare effects[66]. Thus, quoting from its earlier opinion in *Hanson v. Shell Oil.*, the Ninth Circuit in *Janich* reiterated that

> "[t]he antitrust laws were not intended, and may not be used to require businesses to price their products at unreasonably high prices (which penalize the consumer) so that less efficient competitors can stay in business. The Sherman Act is not a subsidy for inefficiency."[67]

The US Supreme Court later echoed this theme in its *Cargill* and *Matsushita* opinions.

Like other early cases adopting the Areeda-Turner test, however, *Janich* contemplates the possibility that, in unusual circumstances, prices exceeding marginal cost may be predatory[68]. Later Ninth Circuit cases maintain, and even extend, this view[69].

William Inglis and Sons Baking Co. v. ITT Continental Baking Co, Inc.[70]

Inglis arose out of the 1976 failure of the Inglis bakery following several years of intense price competition with ITT-Continental in the white bread market in Northern California. This market was marked by over-capacity, stemming in part from the commencement of in-house bread production by supermarket chains. At trial, Inglis persuaded a jury that Continental had, inter alia, engaged in predatory pricing. The trial judge, however, rejected the jury's verdict and the $5 048 000 damage award as clearly contrary to the evidence, and ordered a new trial. On appeal, the Ninth Circuit affirmed in part and reversed in part the trial court's decisions, and remanded the matter for a new trial[71].

While continuing to endorse much of Areeda's and Turner's economic analysis, the *Inglis* decision diverged from the legal standard those commentators had proposed. Instead, the court adopted a burden-shifting approach employing rebuttable presumptions. Under this approach, if the plaintiff demonstrates that the defendant has set prices below average variable cost, the plaintiff has established a prima facie case of predatory pricing, which the defendant may try to rebut[72]. If, however, prices are between average variable and average total cost, the plaintiff bears the burden of demonstrating that the pricing strategy was predatory, i.e., "that the anticipated benefits of defendant's price depended on its tendency to discipline or eliminate competition and thereby enhance the firm's long-term ability to reap the benefits of monopoly power."[73]

The asserted virtue of this approach is that it allows for consideration of non-cost-based evidence to help clarify the intent underlying a firm's pricing behaviour. In the Court's view, this is important because pricing below total cost, while not inherently predatory, may be so under some circumstances. Similarly, under other circumstances, pricing below average variable cost may be a rational, non-predatory, loss-minimizing strategy, particularly during periods of excess capacity or slack demand[74].

Transamerica Computer Co., Inc. v. International Business Machines Corp.[75]

In its 1983 decision in *Transamerica* the Ninth Circuit extended its rebuttable presumption approach to above-total-cost pricing. In this case, the plaintiff challenged as predatory

IBM's strategy to regain market share from firms that, by engaging in reverse engineering, had avoided IBM's research and development costs, and successfully undercut IBM's prices for peripheral equipment products. IBM offered new, lower-priced products (some involving used parts), redesigned the interface between its central processing unit and peripheral equipment (thus making rivals' peripheral equipment incompatible), and offered discounts on long-term leases. The Ninth Circuit affirmed the district court's holding that these actions by IBM had not violated the antitrust laws[76].

The Ninth Circuit decided that prices above average total cost should not be considered lawful per se. Rather, diverging from the Areeda and Turner approach, the Court held that above-cost prices may be unlawful if the plaintiff can demonstrate their predatory character by clear and convincing proof[77]. The court adopted this approach because it envisioned a possibility that above-cost pricing could be exclusionary: for example, where a firm engaged in limit pricing, or dropped its prices to intimidate potential entrants and establish a reputation barrier[78]. The Court also sought to avoid exclusive reliance on cost figures, because such figures are often difficult to compute reliably; and without examining factors such as "intent, market power, market structure, and long run behaviour," the court was hesitant to grant monopolists a "free zone" in which their pricing strategies would be absolved of antitrust scrutiny simply because prices were above average total cost[79]. While other courts have arrived at different determinations concerning whether above-total-cost pricing should be treated as per se lawful, most courts have brought to bear a similar blend of legal, economic, and jurisprudential considerations[80].

Arthur S. Langenderfer, Inc. v. S.E. Johnson Co.[81]

The plaintiff in *Langenderfer*, an asphalt paving company, found itself unable to compete profitably, and was ultimately driven out of business by defendant Johnson, a diversified, vertically-integrated paving firm that had acquired numerous stone quarries and asphalt mixing plants in the area. Defendant's prices, however, were consistently profitable, never dropping below average total cost. The Sixth Circuit Court of Appeals, overturning a $3 000 000 treble damage award and remanding for a new trial, found that plaintiff's problems stemmed from the defendant's greater efficiencies, a problem not remedied by the antitrust laws.

In reaching its decision, the Sixth Circuit criticized the Ninth Circuit's treatment of above-total-cost pricing in *Transamerica*. The court noted that although it had adopted the *Inglis* rule, it would not find prices above average total cost to be predatory, regardless of the defendant's intent to eliminate competition. Such a rule, the court found, would undermine the goals of the antitrust laws — "to promote efficiency, encourage vigorous competition and maximize consumer welfare" — by forcing "a larger, more efficient firm to maintain artificially high prices to the detriment of the public."[82] The Sixth Circuit then endorsed the Seventh Circuit's reasoning that a rule potentially condemning above-total-cost pricing would not only deprive consumers of the benefits of price cuts "by dominant firms facing new competition," but also would "thrust courts into the unseemly position" of monitoring prices to determine which were not profit maximizing[83].

Northeastern Telephone Co. v. AT&T[84]

Northeastern Telephone is significant because it examines competitive issues arising out of the gradual deregulation the American telecommunications industry, and because it

71

emphasizes that a regulated monopolist may respond vigorously to new competition for portions of its business[85]. In this case, the plaintiff, a small supplier of public branch exchanges (PBXs) and other telephone equipment, charged that AT&T and a local affiliate, the Southern New England Telephone Co.(SNET), sought to monopolize the local telephone equipment market. The plaintiff alleged that AT&T required use of an interconnect device that unreasonably disadvantaged Northeastern, that AT&T had engaged in predatory advertising and design changes, and that SNET set prices of its PBXs and telephones at predatorily low levels. At trial, Northeastern won a jury verdict of US$ 16 500 000, after trebling. The Second Circuit Court of Appeals, however, reversed the predatory pricing verdict, and ordered a new trial on the other antitrust claims[86].

The court of appeals closely followed the Areeda-Turner predatory pricing analysis, including particularly its emphasis on short-run welfare maximization and the efficiency benefits of marginal cost pricing[87]. As its predatory pricing test, therefore, the court declared that "prices below reasonably anticipated marginal cost will be presumed predatory, while prices above reasonably anticipated marginal cost will be presumed non-predatory."[88] The court adopted this standard in light of its view that successful predation was rare, and that the high costs of misjudgment make a simple rule especially desirable[89]. Turning to the facts of the case, the court reasoned that since entry barriers into the business telephone equipment market were relatively low, successful remunerative predation was unlikely[90].

The court adopted the marginal cost test notwithstanding that SNET was in part a regulated monopoly and also a multiproduct firm[91]. The plaintiff asserted that a more rigorous test employing an average or fully-distributed cost standard was appropriate because SNET could allocate all joint costs to its monopolized products, thus lowering the variable cost on its unregulated product. The Second Circuit, however, reasoned that diversified firms should be no more likely than single-product firms to engage in predation. Although cross-subsidization could help finance predation, the economic costs to the firm, *i.e.*, the opportunity costs of lost profits, would be the same. The court further noted that an average cost test is more difficult to apply to multi-product firms because the allocation of joint costs is essentially arbitrary. The court preferred, therefore, to let firms allocate joint costs by any "reasonable and consistent method."[92]

The court gave additional reasons for preferring a marginal or average variable cost test, reasons equally applicable to unregulated firms. First, a rule requiring that prices remain above marginal cost would shelter inefficient firms. Second, a fully-distributed cost test would "favour the interests of single market rivals over those of consumers and the competitive process."[93] In this regard, and throughout its opinion, the court gave great weight to the allocative efficiency of marginal cost pricing. Finally, citing considerations of comity and federalism, the court expressed reluctance to impinge on the regulatory agency's function of monitoring SNET's pricing and cost allocations[94].

C. Federal Trade Commission Predatory Pricing Cases

General Foods Corp. [95]

In *General Foods*, the Federal Trade Commission reviewed charges that General Foods had sought to repel competitive efforts by Proctor and Gamble to expand its share of the market for coffee in the eastern United States. The complaint alleged that General Foods, then the dominant producer in that geographic market, had set prices at predatorily low levels, offered excessive promotional allowances, used a "fighting brand," and engaged in geographic price discrimination. The case was tried before an administrative law judge, who determined that General Foods had not violated Section 5 of the Federal Trade Commission

Act or Section 2(a) of the Robinson-Patman Act. On appeal, the Commission viewed its task as determining which had occurred: "rivalry that benefited consumers, or conduct that threatened competition."[96] The Commission found the former, and affirmed the administrative law judge's decision. The Commission's opinion is notable for the two-step approach it adopted for evaluating predatory pricing allegations, and for its detailed analysis of the coffee market, and General Foods' position and prospects within it.

Rather than centre its assessment of the predatory pricing allegations on the element of intent (as in *Inglis*) or on conduct (as in *Northeastern*), the Commission chose to focus first on the element of dangerous probability of success[97]. By doing so, the Commission reserved the more complex questions concerning the respondent's conduct and intent until after determining whether the market was amenable to successful predation. By this two-step approach, the Commission sought both to reach more analytically sound conclusions and to avoid unnecessary expenditure of prosecutorial and administrative resources[98].

The Commission never reached the questions of pricing and intent because it found no dangerous probability that General Foods could "achieve the power to control price or exclude competition in the alleged market(s)."[99] A number of factors supported this conclusion. First, there appeared to be no significant barriers to entry in the regional markets in question; indeed, successful entry had occurred. Second, transshipment in response to small price differentials suggested that the relevant geographic market was considerably larger than the regional ones proposed. Third, the Commission concluded that the high profitability of General Foods' coffee line resulted from superior marketing efficiency and production quality. Because of excess capacity in the industry, the price sensitivity of consumers, and the access by local retailers to outside suppliers, General Foods was seen as having little ability to raise prices, even where it had a large market share[100].

While the *General Foods* case was thus decided on the question of dangerous probability of success, the Commission observed that rigid cost-based rules, such as those in the original Areeda-Turner proposal, posed difficulties. In some situations, pricing below cost might constitute reasonable, non-predatory behaviour. For example, pricing below average variable cost could be an efficient way to create goodwill and stimulate future sales. In such circumstances, the "current" expenditures associated with the promotional effort should properly be amortized over the period during which the promotional effort had its impact. In addition, where business conditions are adverse but exiting and re-entering a market would be costly, a firm might reasonably determine that a wise, loss-minimizing strategy is to remain in the market, sell goods at prevailing (albeit below cost) prices, and accept its losses until conditions change. Thus, the Commission noted with apparent approval a trend in the courts for a rule establishing only a presumption of predation when prices fall below average variable cost, and a "strong, often conclusive, presumption" of legality for prices above average variable cost[101].

International Telephone and Telegraph Corp.[102]

The Commission elaborated its views on the appropriate test for predatory pricing in *ITT*, where complaint counsel contended that ITT's Continental Baking subsidiary had engaged in predatory pricing and discriminatory pricing of bread, in violation of the Federal Trade Commission Act and the Robinson-Patman Act. On appeal, the Commission reversed the administrative law judge's decision finding a violation, and dismissed the complaint.

The Commission's opinion is significant because it expressly articulated the FTC's views concerning the cost standard to be used in evaluating predatory pricing allegations. Initially, the Commission observed that an appropriate rule would satisfy the elements of both predatory intent and predatory conduct. To this end, the Commission concluded that a standard focusing on "sales at prices below the average variable costs of an alleged predator for a significant period of time" could generally serve to distinguish predatory intent and conduct from that which is competitive[103].

The Commission then fashioned a set of three cost-based presumptions embodying this test. First, "[s]ales at prices below average variable cost for a significant period of time should be rebuttably presumed to be anticompetitive."[104] The Commission suggested that defendants might be able to rebut this presumption by demonstrating that the sales were of obsolete, perishable, or otherwise rapidly depreciating goods; that the prices were set at introductory, promotional levels to induce trial purchases; or that the sales were necessary to retain goodwill capital (such a product loyalty) that would be costly to regain if the firm were to exit the market and then re-enter[105]. Second, the Commission decided that sales at or above average variable cost, even though below average total cost, should receive a strong (often conclusive) presumption of legality. The presumption could be rebutted, however, where strong evidence indicates that the sales were inconsistent with profit-maximizing or loss-minimizing strategies[106]. Third, the Commission determined that sales at or above average total cost should be conclusively presumed competitive and lawful. By definition, sales governed by this conclusive presumption could exclude only less efficient firms, an effect that often results from vigorous competition[107].

Even prices classified as "predatory" under these presumptions would not be unlawful, however, unless there was also a dangerous probability that the conduct might result in the acquisition of monopoly power. Therefore, following its *General Foods* approach, the Commission first examined evidence relating to this element, and determined that it was "highly unlikely" that the respondent could have gained market power sufficient to pose a competitive threat. The Commission supported this conclusion by noting ITT's relatively modest share of the relevant markets (ranging from 20 to 30 per cent), the presence of strong competitors, and the lack of substantial entry barriers[108]. Having found no danger of monopolization, the Commission did not evaluate in depth the respondent's pricing behaviour or subjective intent in the context of the attempted monopolization allegations[109].

E. Predatory Pricing under State Law

This summary does not consider predatory pricing cases under state antitrust, loss-leader, price discrimination, and sales below cost statutes. These state statutes frequently are more restrictive than the federal antitrust laws, and thus may prohibit sales that would be permissible under federal law.

12. European Community

A. ECS/AKZO

The 1985 decision by the EC Commission in *ECS/AKZO*[110] is the most recent and significant case including a claim of low pricing to be decided under the Treaty of Rome. That case arose following a complaint by Engineering and Chemical Supplies (Epsom and Gloucester) Ltd (ECS) that it was the victim of a predatory pricing campaign by AKZO Chemie BV which infringed Article 86 of the Treaty. ECS is a small United Kingdom producer of an organic peroxide (benzoyl peroxide) which it sold primarily as a flour additive

74

in the United Kingdom and Ireland, the only states in the EC where such use is permitted. The major use of benzoyl peroxide, however, is in the plastics industry and beginning in 1979 ECS began selling the product to continental European plastics producers. Its major competitor in both the UK flour additives market and in the larger plastics market was AKZO Chemie which is the specialty chemical subsidiary of the large Dutch multinational chemical and fibres group AKZO NV. AKZO held over 50 per cent of the UK flour additives market against ECS's 35 per cent, and a similar share of the overall European organic peroxides market.

ECS' troubles with AKZO started in 1979, when it began its expansion into the plastics market. In meetings with ECS officials, AKZO demanded that ECS withdraw from the plastics market and threatened below cost pricing in the UK flour market if ECS did not comply. ECS then obtained an ex parte injunction against such acts from the High Court in London on the basis that such retaliation would amount to an abuse of dominant position under Article 86 of the Treaty of Rome. This injunction led to a settlement which ran for two and a half years but contained difficult-to-enforce provisions. In 1982, ECS complained to the EC Commission that the practices were continuing, leading to the seizure of AKZO documents and, in 1983, an interim order requiring AKZO to return to earlier profit levels but permitting it to meet competing offers. After the interim measures, AKZO maintained the customers it had won earlier and gained new ones by matching the low bids of Diaflex, the third and smallest firm in the UK flour additives market.

The Commission issued its final decision in 1985, finding abuse of dominant position. The decision is based in part upon AKZO's low pricing and expressed intent to discipline or eliminate ECS but other grounds appear as well, including price discrimination and other non-price exclusionary conduct (e.g., total requirements clauses in its contracts). Notably, the Commission found that AKZO abused not only its dominant position in the UK flour additives market but also in the broader European plastics market, as the conduct in the one market tended to strengthen its dominance in the other by damaging a potentially dangerous new entrant and dissuading others.

The Commission's treatment of AKZO's overall strategy is noteworthy for the standards it creates. Further, given AKZO's defence that its pricing satisfied the Areeda-Turner test of legality, the Commission took up the debate by American academics and applied those concepts to the Treaty of Rome. In particular, the Commission unequivocally rejected the Areeda-Turner test legalizing prices above average variable costs. The Commission held that:

"the standard proposed by AKZO based on a static and short-term conception of 'efficiency' takes no account of the broad objectives of EEC competition rules set out in Article 3(f) and particularly the need to guard against the impairment of an effective structure of competition in the common market. It also fails to take account of the longer-term strategic considerations which may underlie sustained price cutting and which are particularly apparent in the present case. Further it ignores the fundamental importance of the element of discrimination in seeming to permit a dominant manufacturer to recover its full costs from its regular customers while tempting a rival's customers at lower prices. Yet even if the underlying policy considerations of Articles 85 and 86 were limited (as AKZO argues) to the achievement of short-term efficiency, it is not only the 'less efficient' firms which will be harmed if a dominant firm sells below its total cost but above variable cost. If prices are taken to a level where a business does not cover its total costs, smaller but possibly more efficient firms will eventually be eliminated and the larger firm with the greater economic resources - including the possibility of cross-subsidization - will survive."[111]

The Commission went on to state that even pricing above full costs can be anticompetitive. The Commission's dicta on this point is potentially far-reaching:

> "the important element is the rival's assessment of the aggressor's determination to frustrate its expectations, for example as to its rate of growth or attainable profit margins, rather than whether or not the dominant firm covers its own costs. There can thus be an anti-competitive aspect in price cutting whether or not the aggressor sets its prices above or below its own costs (in one or other meaning of the term)."[112]

What emerges is a test which takes costs into account as one factor helping to reveal the reasonableness of pricing conduct and its underlying purpose. If that purpose is to eliminate a competitor or to restrict competition, an infringement of Article 86 is established. This test is qualified, however, by a recognition that even dominant firms can legitimately seek to prevail over rivals, provided that it competes "on the merits" i.e., on the basis of greater efficiency and superior performance[113].

The Commission's decision makes it plain that it found AKZO's pricing unreasonable even under a purely cost-based approach. AKZO's prices to some customers were not only below full cost (which appears to be the Commission's point of departure) but below average variable cost as well. The Commission took particular exception to AKZO's definition of variable costs, which included only raw material and energy costs, noting that direct labour, supervision, repairs, maintenance and royalties should also be included, citing Areeda and Turner's definition, and further noting that Areeda and Turner would exclude only capital costs, certain taxes and depreciation due to obsolesence from variable costs. The fact that AKZO's prices were below variable costs emerged even more strongly when the cost of materials to AKZO UK were examined; the Commission found that artificially low transfer prices were used to cross-subsidize the predatory campaign and to help create the appearance of prices above variable costs.

This below-cost pricing could not be excused by market forces. The UK market did not reflect excess capacity; AKZO's plant was at full capacity, running 24 hours a day. Further, the competition it was purporting to meet seemed artificial; there was some evidence that the low bids by Diaflex, the third firm, were prepared in collusion with AKZO to create the appearance of competition justifying AKZO's low prices.

In addition to this examination of the cost-based evidence, the Commission also relied upon AKZO's clear intent to eliminate ECS, which had been expressed directly to ECS officials and also appeared in internal AKZO documents. This intent was corroborated by an earlier, successful effort by AKZO to limit the growth of another small challenger in the European market. Further evidence of an abuse was found in AKZO's use of price discrimination during the campaign, a practice specifically identified as an abuse under Article 86. AKZO's low bids to ECS' customers were far below the prices AKZO continued to charge its longstanding customers, limiting the losses it suffered during its campaign.

Having found an infringement of Article 86 along with the prerequisite jurisdictional bases, the Commission imposed a fine of 10 million ECU and ordered an end to the infringements, including an end to "unreasonably low" and "artificially low" prices in the UK. Note, however, that AKZO has appealed this decision to the Court of Justice and a ruling on the appeal is expected in the near future.

Discussion

The cases summarized above show how predatory pricing cases have strained courts and competition policy officials across the OECD in their efforts to control abusive pricing without smothering vigorous price competition. The treatment of a number of points could be usefully reviewed at this point: the role of cost-based tests of predation, the additional role of other factors such as intent and non-price conduct, particular problems posed by regulated monopolies and vertically integrated firms, the likelihood of firms conspiring to predate and the role of the predator's market power or likelihood of eventual success.

Concerning the treatment given to the defendant's market power in predation cases a variety of distinct approaches can be seen. The first is that taken by resale-at-a-loss type statutes, where market power is simply not taken into account. Another approach is shown in the US Ninth Circuit decisions in *Janich* and *Inglis* which seem to say that market power can be an element but is not a necessary one; defendant's conduct can make proof of market power unnecessary in appropriate cases. (In *Matsushita* and *Cargill* however the US Supreme Court expressed its view that market power was an important factor, but those cases were disposed of on other issues.) Under German, French and EC competition law, statutory provisions require a focus on market power unless the pricing practices form part of a concerted strategy running afoul of anti-cartel provisions. A strict test of market power is espoused by the US Federal Trade Commission in its *ITT* and *General Foods* decisions, which argue that market power should be looked at first, before attempting to resolve the more difficult issues of the reasonableness of defendant's pricing and intent. Under this view, pricing practices would not be challenged by competition authorities unless it could be established that there was a substantial risk that the alleged predator would acquire or reinforce market power by its efforts to eliminate rivals.

Cost-based predation rules have appeared in practically every jurisdiction considered here, and it is rare for a case to find cost irrelevant in testing for predation. (The principal exception here being the Australian *Victorian Egg Board* case, where costs were disregarded given the non-commercial status of the Board.) Views differ, however, on the relative importance of cost-based criteria vis-à-vis non-cost factors. Different views have been expressed on the types of costs to be considered, on what cost level is the appropriate measure and on what non-cost factors should be considered.

Marginal cost and its surrogate, average variable cost, emerge as a frequently applied test of predation in Member countries, particularly in decisions in the UK such as *Scottish Newspapers*, *Becton Dickinson UK* and *Concrete Roofing Tiles* and in the US, where practically every decision refers to one or the other, e.g., the Ninth Circuit opinions (*Hanson*, *Pacific Engineering*, *Calcomp* and *Inglis*) and the opinions by the FTC (*ITT*, *General Foods*). Average variable cost has also been seen as a relevant measure of predation in the EC in the *AKZO* matter.

Total cost, on the other hand, has seen more limited acceptance as the relevant cost standard, notably in the Swedish *National Telephone Administration* case. It has also been recognized as a relevant measure in the *AKZO* and *Inglis* decisions. Prices above total cost have not been found to be predatory and some decisions, e.g. the FTC in *ITT* and the Court of Appeals in *Langerderfer*, have argued that prices above total cost should be per se legal, but other courts have been reluctant to rule out the possibility of a violation, as in *Inglis* where the Court of Appeals noted the difficulty in apportioning costs in multi-product situations.

A number of decisions recognize that a per se cost-based rule is hazardous. Courts are increasingly finding that low pricing should not be challenged as predatory when economic circumstances can explain price-cutting. The *Inglis* court, for example, noted that prices below total cost can be explained by excess capacity and below average variable costs by re-startup costs. Similar views were expressed in *Pacific Engineering*, *ITT* and in *AB Kronfagel*. Similarly, meeting competition has been recognised as a legitimate reason for price cutting, as in the French *Triponney* decision and in the Australian *CSBP* decision, although the latter case might have been decided differently without the requirement that intent be shown. Other decisions, though, have disallowed a "meeting competition" defence, particularly where the defendant started the price cutting (as in the Swedish *Shell* matter), where the competing offer came from a co-conspirator (as in *AKZO*), or where the pricing was combined with other anticompetitive conduct (as in *Scottish Newspapers*).

The question of intent has arisen in a variety of contexts. Few courts seem willing to disregard evidence of the defendant's intentions but a purely intent-based standard has been criticized both as unworkable (as in *MCI*) and potentially misleading. Rather, evidence on intent is seen as one of the relevant factors in the *AKZO* and the *Victorian Egg Board* decisions. Evidence of an *innocent* intent has been rejected in light of proof of anticompetitive effects (*National Telephone Administration*).

Evidence of predatory intent has been inferred from the pricing behaviour of the firm concerned. For example, the selectivity of price cuts vis-à-vis customers or target markets while high price level are maintained elsewhere has been considered as an expression of predatory intent in certain decisions (*vinegar*, *Dipyridamole*). Non-price conduct has received considerable weight when courts decide whether a pricing practice is to be considered predatory. A number of French decisions show how non-price conduct can illuminate the meaning of price-cutting. Thus price-cutting has been weighed in light of the defendant's concurrent use of litigation against the victim (in the *vinegar* matter), of exclusionary long-term contracts with customers (in *industrial gases*) and breaking contracts and intervening before regulatory authorities (in *Dipyridamole*). Similar weight to exclusionary non-price conduct was given by the Office of Fair Trading in the *Scottish Newspapers* investigation where the predator sought exclusive advertising contracts and tried to block the printing of the rival paper.

The difficult problems raised when regulated monopolies also engage in competitive lines of business have received differing treatments by reviewing authorities. The Swedish Market Court's concern over cross-subsidization in the *National Telephone Authority* case led to a view that the cross-subsidy could be avoided only by an allocation of all costs between NTA's various lines of business, that separate accounting was desirable and that competitive subsidiaries should be spun off where possible. In the *Northeastern Telephone* decision, however, a similar allocation of all costs was criticized as arbitrary and economically irrelevant and an incremental cost standard applied instead.

The risk of cross-subsidies by vertically-integrated firms has also received some attention. Most authorities recognize that vertically integrated firms do have the ability to subsidize predatory efforts through unrealistic transfer pricing and that such pricing can make rigid reliance on a cost-based measure unreasonable. The EC Commission in *AKZO* and the French Competition Commission in *dipyridamole* and *reinforcing bars* expressed their scepticism over the transfer prices used in those cases. On the other hand, the US Sixth Circuit Court of Appeals appeared to simply accept defendant's transfer prices in its *Langenderfer* decision and attributed the defendant's lower prices to its greater efficiency as a vertically integrated firm.

The implausibility of plaintiff's predation conspiracy theory was a major factor in the Supreme Court's decision in *Matsushita*, yet just such a conspiracy was uncovered in France in the *intravenous solutions* matter. The latter case however also involved a fairly well developed cartel among the nine defendant firms and some practices by their customers and trade association which facilitated the cartel's operation.

A final point is to note the manner in which various courts have considered the academic proposals which were summarized in Chapter 4 above. The Areeda-Turner rule quickly set the terms of the debate in the US and elsewhere but courts have generally moved away from its original per se proscriptions. On the other hand, writers like Baumol (who would regulate future price rises) and Williamson (output expansion) have seen their proposals essentially ignored in subsequent decisions. McGee and Easterbrook have not seen their no-rule approach adopted in any decision but their arguments concerning the frequency of predation and the risk that a restrictive rule will harm price competition have influenced both the US Supreme Court and US Federal Trade Commission. Finally, Joskow and Klevorick's two-tier approach has at least in part been incorporated in recent US Federal Trade Commission decisions.

VII.   CONCLUSIONS

Predatory pricing refers to the use of short-run price-cutting in an effort to exclude rivals on a basis other than efficiency in order to gain or protect market power. It has been of concern to competition policy officials since the passage of the first antitrust laws and continues to be so in many jurisdictions. Competition policy officials often receive complaints of predatory pricing by self-described "prey" and private actions continue to be filed where they are permitted. Moreover, with the recent movement to deregulate or privatise many dominant firms, there is concern that predatory pricing practices will become more frequent in the future. Interest in predatory pricing rules has also heightened recently because of its possible application to international trade in that clearly thought-out competition rules could help illuminate or even supplant rules governing dumping.

Predatory pricing, however, is a complex form of anticompetitive conduct. It requires the perpetrator to incur substantial losses or at least to forego present profits in the hope that those losses can be more than recouped in the future through the exercise of market power. Thus market conditions play a key role in determining whether price predation is a feasible tactic for a firm to employ. The predator must have a very substantial share of the market or at least the capacity to acquire such a share. In addition, entry conditions must be such that market power can be exercised for some period of time following a predatory episode in order to provide recoupment for the predator's "investment". To the extent that a predator mistakes market conditions his self-inflicted losses will not be regained and in this sense predation can be said to be self-deterring.

There has been considerable debate over the frequency with which predation occurs and thus the appropriate type of rule, if any, which should be used to control it. Unfortunately, the precise frequency with which predation occurs remains unknown as no reliable statistics are available. Recently, predation has been alleged with less frequency in certain US courts, and the decreasing frequency there may merely reflect the rise of the Areeda-Turner rule, which is relatively hostile to plaintiffs. Studies of celebrated cases have also appeared but provide little basis for extrapolation to other firms' practices. A further difficulty is the fact that legal and market conditions can vary significantly from country to country, adding to the risks of extrapolation.

Perhaps all that can be said is that cases of predation may arise but at most only very infrequently. Complaints of predation, however, are presented to competition authorities with some regularity, although the great majority of these cases involve nothing more than healthy price competition. Thus competition authorities need some method to separate systematically the occasional violation from numerous complaints.

Such a rule should thus be able to identify predatory pricing when it occurs yet impose little or no restraint on the ability of firms to compete vigorously on price. These potentially conflicting requirements demand a cautious approach in developing a minimally restrictive rule. Any rule, moreover, should provide clear guidance to the business community in order to encourage price competition and limit abusive litigation.

Predation rules such as the one suggested below are not the only mechanism by which competition authorities can attack predatory pricing. Predatory pricing can only succeed when markets do not function properly. Efforts by competition authorities to encourage and protect competitive market conditions should limit the possibility for successful predation. Thus efforts to improve the conditions for entry and expansion in a given market, including the removal of barriers to international competition, should help combat the threat of effective predation.

One promising line of action against predatory pricing is the "two-tier" approach under which competition authorities would look first to the market in question and determine whether it is susceptible to successful predation. This could involve a quick inquiry into product and geographic market definitions and entry conditions under supra-competitive pricing. If it appeared unlikely due to market structure and entry conditions that the alleged predator would be able to exercise market power in the post-predation period, the inquiry should end, as there would be no harm to competition even if some competitors suffered during the price-cutting episode. In a similar vein, current rules prohibiting sales below some cost floor without regard to market conditions could be reconsidered, as such rules likely inhibit some measure of pro-competitive price-cutting.

For those cases which survive the first tier, a multifaceted inquiry would be appropriate. The main focus of this second stage should be on prices in relation to costs in light of the economic context. In conducting this inquiry there should be no single bright line below which a price is necessarily predatory; even free goods can be justified in certain circumstances. Competition authorities thus should consider what factors justify sharp price-cutting:

a) Prices above total cost should not be considered to be predatory. Numerous decisions have noted that a rule requiring prices above total costs will tend to protect inefficient producers.

b) Pricing between average variable and average total costs, even though not sustainable in the long run, can be economically sound and non-predatory in a variety of circumstances. For example, such pricing can be non-predatory when there is excess capacity for whatever reason or when there are goods which must be cleared out, e.g. due to obsolecence, the risk of spoilage or shifting consumer tastes. The pressure of competition in a particular market may also produce prices in this range, thus the fact that price differentials exist across markets may indicate merely differing levels of competition and not necessarily predation.

c) Even prices below average variable costs may be economically justified, e.g. when there are circumstances as described in the preceding paragraph and re-startup costs which make below average cost pricing the loss-minimizing choice. In addition, new entrants in a market should be given great freedom in their pricing decisions in order to induce purchasers to change their habits or to gain economies of scale. Similar latitude should be given to the pricing of a new product, where initially low prices can be justified by the need to gain manufacturing experience and volume.

The question of how costs should be defined has no easy answer; the case-by-case approach adopted by some courts seems to be the most pragmatic solution. However, costs may be misrepresented by a predator and the adoption of cost-based rules will likely encourage the use of creative accounting techniques. Of particular concern here is the transfer pricing of a vertically-integrated firm and the allocation of costs by multiproduct firms. The opportunity for such firms to disguise predatory activities both increases the likelihood that the predation will succeed (because of asymmetry of information) and that it will go unpunished (because prices will appear to be above costs). Thus courts and competition authorities need to pay careful attention to purported costs and not hesitate to disregard cost figures which seem to be unrealistic.

If prices seem fully justified in relation to costs and economic conditions, the inquiry should end. There seems to be little point in inquiring into intent when pricing can be fully explained by the objective economic circumstances. Further, such an inquiry could produce anomalous results. For example, it would make little sense to prosecute someone with "bad" intent when no liability would attach to the same pricing by someone with other intentions. Rather, intent and other factors would seem to be useful only when the price-cost comparison is ambiguous, e.g. when cost allocations are uncertain or the economic setting unclear.

If intent is thus brought into the inquiry, documentary evidence of the state-of-mind of the responsible company officials can be relevant. Such evidence, however, should not be required as any well-counselled firm can assure that no such material will be found. A better method of discovering the intentions of the alleged firm would be to examine its actions. In some cases, non-price anti-competitive conduct will be found alongside pricing conduct and such non-price activities should be a relatively reliable guide to the defendant's true goals. Examples of such non-price conduct could include harassing litigation against the prey, intervention before regulatory agencies, interference with the prey's business relations with its suppliers or customers and otherwise inexplicable shifts to requirements contracts or exclusive dealing arrangements.

This second stage of the inquiry, while potentially broader than a simple price-cost comparison, is narrower than an "all factors" approach suggested by some commentators. There is considerable risk that such an open-ended investigation could bog down, overwhelmed by myriad complex lines of possible inquiry.

Price predation may not be the only tactic used by a firm seeking market power. Non-price predation, also known as raising rivals' costs, may also be employed either in conjunction with a price-cutting campaign or independently. This report has briefly described the theory of non-price predation to show how it could accompany a price-based campaign. Moreover, an overly restrictive pricing rule could be misused by a non-price predator to restrain or discipline rivals. Because non-price predation is not premised upon present losses by the predator against the possibility of future gains - indeed, the gains may be immediate - the practice may be more pervasive than predatory pricing alone. Further, non-price predation could be employed as an instrument of protectionism by a domestic firm seeking to limit international competition, e.g. by embroiling the would-be importer in costly litigation or by petitioning government agencies to effectively block imports. Note, however, that the notion of non-price predation is not simple and truly pro-competitive activities, e.g. product innovation, could be misconstrued as non-price predation. Thus it is a theory to be applied carefully.

NOTES AND REFERENCES

II

1. Richard A. Posner, *Antitrust Law -- An Economic Perspective*, at 185-186 (1976).

2. F. Scherer, *Industrial Market Structures and Economic Performance*, at 338, (2nd Edition, 1980).

3. John S. McGee, *Predatory Pricing Revisited*, 23 Journal of Law and Economics 289 (1980).

4. Frank H. Easterbrook, *Predatory Strategies and Counterstrategies*, 48 University of Chicago Law Review 263 (1981).

5. McGee, supra note 3 at pages 295-298.

6. Id. at 299, 311.

7. Id. at 292 and note 14.

8. Easterbrook, supra note 4.

9. Id. at 272-275.

10. Id. at 282-286.

11. McGee, supra note 3 at 310-311; Easterbrook, supra note 4 at 292-293.

12. Richard Selten, *The Chain Store Paradox*, 9 Theory and Decision 127, 131 (1978).

13. Id. at 132-133.

14. Id. at 152-153.

15. Paul Milgrom and John Roberts, *Predation, Reputation and Entry Deterrence*, 27 Journal of Economic Theory 280, 284-285 (1982).

16. Id. at 302-303.

17. Id. at 303-304.

18. Easterbrook, supra note 4 at 286.

19. Schwarz, *Wirtschaft und Wettbewerb* 1987, at 93 et seq.

20. David M. Kreps and Robert Wilson, *Reputation and Imperfect Information*, 27 Journal of Economic Theory 253 (1981).

21. James G. Miller, "Predation: The Changing View in Economics and the Law", remarks before the Antitrust and Economic Efficiency Conference, Hoover Institution, Stanford, California, 30th August 1984, at page 3.

22. Consider, for example, what would happen to a firm schooled in McGee's arguments. It enters, expecting the bluff to unravel and the predation to stop. The established firm, however, is either truly more efficient, and the entrant loses, or is committed to predate to protect other markets, and

the entrant again loses. It would seem that something more than toughness, perversity perhaps, would be required for an entrant to continue in such an endeavour.

23. They find that the Milgrom and Roberts and Kreps and Wilson models:

    "significantly restrict the strategies available to the players. In each period a new market appears. They require that predation, once it has begun in any market must continue in that market, so formally they have a series of one shot games. Since giving up is not permitted, predation, once started, is automatically credible for any market. The classical question [cf. Telser (1966), McGee (1980)], 'How long can it pay to prey?' is swept aside."

    David Easly, Robert Masson and Robert Reynolds, *Preying for Time*, 33 Journal of Industrial Economy 443, 447 (1985).

24. Id. at 453.

25. Irwin M. Stelzer, "Changing Antitrust Standard", remarks before the Workshop on Antitrust Issues in Today's Economy, the Conference Board, New York, 5th March 1987, at page 5.

26. Robert Bork, *The Antitrust Paradox: A Policy at War with Itself* at 155-160, 347-348.

27. Id.

28. Terry Calvani and Randolph W. Tritell, *Invocation of United States Import Relief Laws as an Antitrust Violation*. Remarks before the Fordham Corporate Law Institute (1985), reprinted in 16 Journal of Reprints for Antitrust Law and Economics 475, 476-477.

29. Spencer Weber Waller, *The Collusive Settlement of International Trade Cases*, 16 Journal of Reprints for Antitrust Law and Economics 505, 507-511 (1986).

30. Janusz A. Ordover and Robert D. Willig, *An Economic Definition of Predation: Pricing and Product Innovation*, 91 Yale Law Journal 8, 9 (1981).

31. See, e.g., *Predation, Strategy and Antitrust Analysis*, S. Salop, ed., Federal Trade Commission (1981); S. Salop and D. Scheffman, *Raising Rivals' Costs* 73 American Economic Review 267 (1983); S. Salop and D. Scheffman, *A Bidding Analysis of Special Interest Regulation: Raising Rivals' Costs in a Rent Seeking Society*, Working Paper, Federal Trade Commission Bureau of Economics (1984); *Competition and Cooperation in the Market for (Veritical) Exclusionary Rights*, 76 American Economics Review 109 (1986); and T.G. Krattenmaker and S. Salop, *Anticompetitive Exclusion: Raising Rivals' Costs to Achieve Power over Price*, 96 Yale Law Journal 209 (1986).

32. See Salop, *Raising Rivals Costs*, supra note 31 at 267-268.

33. Salop and Krattenmaker, supra note 31 at 209-211.

34. Id. at 231-242.

35. T.J. Brennen, *Understanding "Raising Rivals' Costs"*, US Department of Justice Discussion Paper EAG 86-16 (1986).

36. Id. at 23.

37. Id.

38. See Richard Craswell and Mark R. Fratrik, *Predatory Pricing Theory Applied; The Case of Supermarkets vs. Warehouse Stores*, 36 Case Western Law Rev. 1 (1986).

III

1. John S. McGee, *Predatory Price Cutting: The Standard Oil (N.J.) Case*, 1 Journal of Law and Economics 137 (1958).

2. John S. McGee, *Predatory Pricing Revisited*, 23 Journal of Law and Economics 289, at 291-292.

3. Id. Note that such "no-rule" proposals refer to specific rules against predatory pricing. These should not be misconstrued as arguments against the existence of more general competition law provisions, such as provisions against the abuse of a dominant position.

4. Kenneth G. Elzinga, *Predatory Pricing: The Case of the Gunpowder Trust*, 13 Journal of Law and Economics 223 (1970).

5. B.S. Yamey, *Predatory Price Cutting: Notes and Comments*, 15 Journal of Law and Economics 129 (1972).

6. Malcom Burns, *Predatory Pricing and the Acquisition Costs of Competitors*, 94 Journal of Political Economy 266 (1986).

7. Id. at 289-290.

8. R. Mark Issac and Vernon L. Smith, *In Search of Predatory Pricing*, 93 Journal of Political Economy 320 (1985).

9. Id. at 334-338.

10. Steven C. Salop and Lawrence J. White, *Economic Analysis of Private Antitrust Litigation*, 74 Georgetown Law Journal 1001 (1986).

11. Id. at 1008.

IV

1. For example, Easterbrook has estimated that the "average" predation case in the United States cost $5-10 million to litigate, *Strategy, Predation and Antitrust Analysis* (1981, S. Salop, ed.) at 640, and has elsewhere reported that AT & T spent $100 million *annually* to defend against charges of predation, Easterbrook, *Predatory Strategies and Counterstrategies*, 48 U. Chicago Law Rev. 263, 334 (1981).

2. See Waller, supra Ch. 2 note 29.

3. See eg., Easterbrook, *Predatory Strategies*, supra note 1 at 264, 333-37 (1981); John McGee, *Predatory Pricing Revisited*, 23 J. of Law and Econ. 289, 316-17 (1980).

4. Easterbrook, *Predatory Strategies*, supra note 1 at 336-37 (emphasis in original).

5. Philip Areeda and Donald F. Turner, *Predatory Pricing and Related Practices Under Section 2 of the Sherman Act*, 88 Harvard Law Review 697 (1975).

6. Areeda and Turner, 3 *Antitrust Law* 148 (1978).

7. Areeda and Turner, 3 *Antitrust Law* 114 (1982 Supplement).

8. Areeda and Hovencamp, 3 *Antitrust Law* 329 (1986 Supplement).

9. Areeda and Turner, *Predatory Pricing*, supra note 5 at 698-99.

10. Id. at 699.

11. Areeda and Turner, *Antitrust Law*, supra note 7 at 127-129.

12. Areeda and Turner, *Antitrust Law*, supra note 6 at 166.

13. Eg., Areeda and Turner, *Predatory Pricing*, supra note 5 at 711.

14. Areeda and Turner, *Antitrust Law*, supra note 6 at 159-161.

15. Id.

16. Areeda and Turner, *Predatory Pricing*, supra note 5 at 716.

17. Areeda and Hovencamp, *Antitrust Law*, supra note 8 at 359-60, 389-90, 393-96.

18. Areeda and Turner, *Antitrust Law*, supra note 6 at 153.

19. Areeda and Turner, *Predatory Pricing*, supra note 5 at 704-706.

20. Id. at 709-710.

21. Id. at 733.

22. Id. at 713-716.

23. Areeda and Hovencamp, *Antitrust Law*, supra note 8 at 409-12.

24. Areeda and Turner, *Antitrust Law*, supra note 6 at 154.

25. Areeda and Turner, *Antitrust Law*, supra note 7 at 119; Areeda and Hovencamp, *Antitrust Law*, supra note 8 at 337.

26. E.g., Areeda and Hovencamp, *Antitrust Law*, supra note 8 at 335-36. The only exception they can see is the case where marginal costs substantially exceed average costs because the plant is greatly exceeding its capacity, a situation which would not harm equally efficient rivals and be so rare it could be ignored. Id. at 405.

27. Areeda and Turner, *Antitrust Law*, supra note 6 at 174.

28. Id. at 176.

29. Id. at 154, 176-78.

30. Richard Posner, *Antitrust Law: An Economic Perspective* 191-192 (1976).

31. Id. at 190.

32. Id. at 55-60, 191.

33. Id. at 189-90.

34. Id. at 193.

35. Oliver E. Williamson, *Predatory Pricing: A Strategic and Welfare Analysis*, 87 Yale Law Journal 284 (1977).

36. Id. at 293.

37. Id. at 299-301.

38. Id.

39. Id. at 297-302.

40. Id. at 296.

41. Id. at 299.

42. Id. at 307-08.

43. Id. at 309-10.

44. The measure is not simply past output but a projection of future demand based on past demand and he would add a 10 per cent leeway for the dominant firm. Id. at 305-06. Areeda and Turner suggest however that this margin could eliminate the incentives for the firm to produce more pre-entry. Philip Areeda and Donald Turner, *Williamson on Predatory Pricing*, 87 Yale Law Journal 1337, 1347 (1978).

45. Id. at 333-34.

46. Williamson adds on top of these rules other cost-based rules which would apply to firms in "loose oligopoly" apparently when no entry is occurring. These rules would require prices at or above short-run average costs in the "intermediate run" and at or above full cost in the long-run. Two major exceptions are that "occasional price wars of very limited duration" would be permitted (but successive ones would be considered together) and that prices could drop to average variable cost in cases of chronic excess supply. Id. at 336-37.

47. McGee, supra note 3.

48. Areeda and Turner, *Williamson on Predatory Pricing*, 87 Yale Law Journal 1337 (1978).

49. McGee, supra note 3 at 310-14.

50. Id. at 313.

51. See discussion Chapter 2 supra.

52. Areeda and Turner, note 48 supra at 1343-44.

53. Id.

54. Id. at 1345-47.

55. See, eg., Oliver Williamson, *Williamson on Predatory Pricing II*, 88 Yale Law Journal 1183, 1188-89 (1979).

56. William Baumol, *Quasi-Permanence of Price Reductions: A Policy for Prevention of Predatory Pricing*, 89 Yale Law Journal 1 (1979).

57. Id. at 4-8.

58. Id. at 6-7.

59. Areeda and Turner, *Antitrust Law*, supra note 7.

60. Richard Craswell and Mark Fratrik, *Predatory Price Theory Applied: The Case of Supermarkets vs. Warehouse Stores*, 36 Case Western Reserve Law Review 1 (1986).

61. Id. at 21-22.

62. Id.

63. Id. at 33.

64. Id. at 47.

65. Id. at 29-31.

66. Id. at 32-33.

67. Id. at 47-48.

68. Id. at 40-46.

69. Id. at 47-48.

70. Areeda and Turner, *Antitrust Law*, supra note 7 at 123-24.

71. F.M. Sherer, *Predatory Pricing and the Sherman Act: A Comment*, 89 Harvard Law Review 869 (1976).

72. Id. at 871-73.

73. Id. at 874.

74. Id. at 890.

75. Louis Phlips, *Predatory Pricing* (EC Commission, 1987).

76. Id. at 67-68.

77. Id. at 69.

78. Schwarz, *Wirtschaft und Wetteberb* 1987, at 93 et seq.

79. Stelzer, supra Ch. 2 note 25 at 7.

80. Paul Joskow and Alvin Klevorik, *A Framework for Analysing Predatory Pricing Policy*, 89 Yale Law Journal 213 (1979).

81. Id. at 242-44.

82. Id. at 244.

83. Id. at 225-234.

84. Id. at 245.

85. Areeda and Hovencamp, *Antitrust Law*, supra note 8 at 341.

86. Id. at 343-46.

87. Joskow and Klevorik, supra note 80 at 249-57.

88. Areeda and Turner, *Antitrust Law*, supra note 6 at 173.

89. Id. at 173-74.

V

1. 4 Bulletin de la Réglementation Commerciale, Ministry of Economic Affairs, (August 1973).

2. Id. at 16-17.

3. Id. at 10.

4. Id. at 7.

5. Section 2(1) The Monopolies and Restrictive Practices Supervision Act (Statute No. 102 of 31st March 1955).

6. Id. at Section 11(1).

7. Id. at Section 11(2).

8. Id. at Section 12(1-2).

9. Although this discussion considers only federal law, predatory pricing is also subject to the antitrust and trade practices laws of individual states. Some states, for example, mandate minimum mark-ups for specified goods, and others prohibit below cost sales. Thus, conduct permitted under federal law may be proscribed by the laws of a particular state. In addition, conduct by private parties that would otherwise violate federal antitrust law may nonetheless be immune from federal challenge under the "state action" doctrine, *Parker v. Brown*, 317 US 341 (1943), if the challenged restraint reflects "clearly articulated and affirmatively expressed" state policy, and the anticompetitive conduct is "actively supervised" by the state itself. *California Retail Liquor Dealers Assn. v. Midcal Aluminum, Inc.*, 445 US 97, 105 (1980) (quoting *Lafayette v. Louisiana Power & Light Co.* 435 US 389, 410 (1978)).

10. 15 USC Section 2.

11. Although predatory pricing is thought more commonly to be single firm conduct, cases involving conspiracy allegations do arise. See, e.g., *Matsushita Electrical Industrial Co., Ltd v. Zenith Radio Corp*, 475 US 574, 590 (1986). (Predatory pricing schemes are "incalculably more difficult to execute than an analogous plan undertaken by a single predator.") In these instances, Section 1 of the Sherman Act, 15 USC Section 1, which prohibits combinations or conspiracies in restraint of trade, may be used to challenge the practice.

12. 15 USC Section 13(a).

13. Secondary line discrimination (which injures the rivals of favoured customers) and tertiary line discrimination (which injures the rivals of firms that purchase from favoured customers) are not so clearly predatory, in the usual meaning of that term.

14. 15 USC Sections 4, 16.

15. 15 USC Section 45(a)(1).

16. Although the Federal Trade Commission enforces the Sherman Act only through Section 5 of the Federal Trade Commission Act (i.e., conduct that violates the Sherman Act also violates Section 5

of the FTC Act), the Commission may enforce the Clayton Act either directly or through the FTC Act. 15 USC Section 21.

The Federal Trade Commission typically has not gone to federal court first in predatory pricing cases. Rather, the prevailing (as well as traditional) approach is that the case is presented initially to an administrative law judge, whose opinion may subsequently be reviewed by the Commission. Parties who appeal from a Commission decision present their case directly to a federal Court of Appeals, without going to a federal District Court.

17. *General Foods Corporation*, 103 FTC 204, 365 (1984). Section 5 of the FTC Act permits the Commission to challenge practices that violate the basic policies of the antitrust laws even if those acts do not actually violate the Sherman or Clayton Act. *FTC v. Sperry & Hutchinson Co.*, 405 US 233 (1972). The Commission has determined, however, that it should treat predatory pricing under Section 5 of the FTC Act according to the same standards that are applied to such conduct under Section 2 of the Sherman Act. *General Foods*, 103 FTC at 365.

18. 384 US 563, 570-71 (1966).

19. *United States v. E.I. du Pont de Nemours & Co.*, 351 US 377, 391 (1956).

20. *Grinnell*, 384 US at 570-71; *Berkey Photo, Inc. v. Eastman Kodak Company*, 603 F.2d 263, 275 (2d Cir. 1979), *cert. denied*, 444 US 1093 (1980).

21. *Berkey* 603 F.2d at 281.

22. As the First Circuit noted in *Barry Wright Corp. v. ITT Grinnell Corp.*, 724 F.2d 227 (1st Cir. 1983):

"'Exclusionary' conduct is conduct, other than competition on the merits or restraints reasonably 'necessary' to competition on the merits, that reasonably appears capable of making a significant contribution to creating or maintaining monopoly power."

Id., at 230 (quoting III P. Areeda and D. Turner, *Antitrust Law* at 83 (1978)).

23. See, e.g., *Aspen Skiing Co. v. Aspen Highlands Skiing Corp.*, 472 US 585, 605 (1985) ("In addition, it is relevant to consider [the challenged conduct's] impact on consumers and whether it has impaired competition in an unnecessarily restrictive way".)

24. These elements are derived from the seminal formulation in *Swift & Co. v. US*, 196 US 375, 396 (1905) ("Where acts are not sufficient in themselves to produce a result which the law seeks to prevent — for instance, the monopoly — but require further acts in addition to the mere forces of nature to bring that result to pass, an intent to bring it to pass is necessary in order to produce a dangerous probability that it will happen."). Most courts now adopt this three-element approach. See, e.g., *International Tel. & Tel. Co.*, 104 FTC 280, 400 n.23 (1984) and cases cited therein. Some courts, however, inferring a firm's intent from its conduct, may define the offence of attempted monopolization as having only two elements (dangerous probability of success and unlawful intent), and treat questions of intent and conduct simultaneously. *McGahee v. Northern Propane Gas Co.*, 55 Antitrust & Trade Reg. Rep. (BNA) 818, 819 (11th Cir. Oct. 27, 1988); *National Reporting Co. v. Alderson Reporting Co.*, 763 F.2d 1020, 1025 (8th Cir. 1985); *Adjusters Replace-A-Car v. Agency Rent-A-Car, Inc.*, 735 F.2d 884, 887 (5th Cir. 1984), *cert. denied*, 469 US 1160 (1985). *See also Shoppin' Bag of Pueblo, Inc. v. Dillon Companies, Inc.*, 783 F.2d 159 (10th Cir. 1986), which articulates proof of relevant geographic and product markets as a fourth element.

25. *Transamerica Computer Co., Inc. v. IBM Corp.*, 698 F.2d 1377, 1382 (9th Cir.), *cert. denied*, 464 US 955 (1983). *Accord Barry Wright Corp. v. ITT Grinnell Corp.*, 724 F.2d 227, 239 (1st Cir. 1983).

26. *International Telephone & Telegraph Corp.*, 104 FTC 280, 396 (1984).

27. *ITT*, 104 FTC at 401 (quoting *E.I. Du Pont de Nemours & Co.*, 96 FTC 653, 738-39 (1980)).

28. Rule, "Claims of Predation in a Competitive Marketplace: When is an Antitrust Response Appropriate" Remarks at the American Bar Association Annual Meeting 5 (9th August 1988).

29. *Times Picayune Publishing Co. v. United States*, 345 US 594, 626 (1953).

30. *ITT*, 104 FTC at 401 (quoting *General Foods Corp.*, 103 FTC at 341-42).

31. See, e.g., *International Telephone and Telegraph*, 104 FTC 280, 396 (1984); *William Inglis & Sons Baking Co. v. ITT Continental Baking Co., Inc.*, 668 F.2d 1014, 1028) (9th Cir. 1981), *cert. denied*, 459 US 825 (1982) (although improper intent may be inferred from clearly threatening or exclusionary conduct, "direct evidence of intent alone, without corroborating evidence of conduct, cannot sustain a claim of attempted monopolization"). *See also* R. Bork, *The Antitrust Paradox* at 144 (1978); L. Sullivan, *Antitrust* at 135-136 (1977).

32. See, e.g., *Northeastern Telephone Co. v. AT&T*, 651 F.2d 76 (2d Cir. 1981), *cert. denied*, 455 US 943 (1982); *International Air Industries v. American Excelsior Co.*, 517 F.2d 714 (5th Cir. 1975), *cert. denied*, 424 US 943 (1976).

33. See, e.g., *Instructional Systems Development Corp. v. Aetna Casualty and Surety Co.*, 817 F.2d 639, 648 (10th Cir. 1987); *McGahee v. Northern Propane Gas Co.*, 55 Antitrust & Trade Reg. Rep. (BNA) 818, 823 (11th Cir. 27th October 1988).

34. Rule, "Claims of Predation in a Competitive Marketplace: When is an Antitrust Response Appropriate" Remarks at the American Bar Association Annual Meeting 14 (9th August 1988).

35. See, e.g., *Cargill, Inc. v. Monfort of Colorado, Inc.*, 479 US 104, 119 n.15 (noting two different commentators that suggest that predation is unlikely with less than a 60 per cent market share, but also noting that a firm with a low market share and substantial excess capacity might be able to absorb quickly its rivals' market shares); *McGahee v. Northern Propane Gas Co.*, 55 Antitrust & Trade Reg. Rep. (BNA) 818, 825-26 (11th Cir. 27th October 1988) (65 per cent market share sufficient to create genuine issue of fact concerning dangerous probability of success); *General Foods*, 103 FTC at 345. *See also Antitrust Law Developments (Second)* 140-142 (J. Loftis ed. 1984) and cases cited therein.

36. *ITT*, 104 FTC at 412 (quoting *General Foods Corp.*, 103 FTC at 345.) See also *Antitrust Law Developments (Second)* II-7-8 (Supp. II 1986); but cf. *McGahee v. Northern Propane Gas Co.*, 55 Antitrust & Trade Reg. Rep. (BNA) 818, 826 (11th Cir. 27th October 1988) (viewing market share as the best indicator of market power).

    The dangerous probability of success element has been a source of controversy. The majority view requires a specific showing that the predator has a dangerous probability of obtaining monopoly power in some market. By contrast, the Ninth Circuit asserts that the purpose of the dangerous probability of success element is not to establish the likelihood of competitive injury in some well defined market, but rather to reflect on the alleged predator's intent. *Inglis*, 668 F.2d at 1029. The Ninth Circuit holds, therefore, that market power, while relevant in establishing a dangerous probability of success, is not essential. Rather, "a dangerous probability of success may be inferred either (1) from direct evidence of specific intent plus proof of conduct directed to accomplishing the unlawful design, or (2) from evidence of conduct alone, provided the conduct is also the sort from which the specific intent can be inferred." *Inglis*, 668 F.2d at 1029 (footnotes omitted). This latter category includes conduct either that forms "the basis for a substantial claim of restraint of trade," or that "is clearly threatening to competition or clearly exclusionary." Id. at n.11. Thus, the Ninth Circuit's "double inference" approach can remove the necessity for a plaintiff to define markets and prove market power in some circumstances, and may allow Section 2 of the Sherman Act to reach firms with under 40 per cent market shares that engage in anticompetitive conduct. *Accord Shoppin' Bag of Pueblo, Inc. v. Dillon Companies*, 783 F.2d 159, 163 (10th Cir. 1986) ("In substance, the [Ninth Circuit and Tenth Circuit] tests for dangerous probability are very much alike."); *Contra McGahee*, 55 Antitrust & Trade Reg. Rep. at 825; *International Distribution Centers, Inc. v. Walsh Trucking Co., Inc.*, 812 F.2d 786, 790-91 (2d Cir. 1987) (expressly rejecting Ninth Circuit approach). See generally *Antitrust Law Developments* 140-44; *Antitrust Law Developments* Ch. IIC (1984 & Supp. II 1988).

37. *Cargill, Inc. v. Monfort of Colorado, Inc.*, 479 US 104, 122 n.17 (1986).

38. Id. (*quoting Matsushita Electric Industrial Co., Ltd. v. Zenith Radio Corp.*, 475 US 574, 594

(1986)). *See also Barry Wright Corp. v. ITT Grinnell Corp.*, 724 F.2d 227, 234 (1st Cir. 1983) ("[W]e must be concerned lest a rule or precedent that authorizes a search for a particular type of undesirable pricing behaviour ends up by discouraging legitimate pricing competition."). As the Assistant Attorney General in charge of the Antitrust Division of the US Department of Justice explained recently:

> "Distinguishing between efficient and inefficient competition is very difficult, if not impossible, because anticompetitive strategic behaviour on its face is often so similar to vigorous competition and the exercise of good business judgment. Practices that raise suspicions of predation, such as cutting price to rock bottom, building a higher fixed cost/lower variable cost plant than is the industry norm, or locking up long-term supplies or outlets, also can represent efficient business decisions in response to changing market conditions. Even under the best of circumstances, the ability of enforcers and courts to obtain and evaluate information is simply not adequate to distinguish reliably between efficient and inefficient competition."

Rule, "Claims of Predation in a Competitive Marketplace: When is an Antitrust Response Appropriate" Remarks at the American Bar Association Annual Meeting 13 (9th August 1988).

39. *Antitrust Law Developments (Second)* at 222.

40. 15 USC Sections 15(a), (b).

41. See, e.g., *Inglis*, 668 F.2d at 1042, which describes these differences, but follows the majority approach that price cuts failing to raise a dangerous probability of success also will not threaten to lessen competition.

42. See *Antitrust Law Developments (Second)* at 231-34.

43. *Henry v. Chloride, Inc.*, 809 F.2d 1334, 1341, 1344 (8th Cir. 1987). Similarly, in *General Foods*, 103 FTC at 357, the Federal Trade Commission explained:

The same facts that reveal a dangerous probability of successful monopolization will indicate a lessening of competition or a tendency to create a monopoly. Since both statutes are directed towards the same goal — the protection of competition — it follows that the inquiries under each should be the same.

44. The Eighth Circuit in *Henry v. Chloride* found support for this approach in the Supreme Court's *Matsushita* opinion, which emphasized the question of whether predatory pricing would be profitable in the given market.

45. See *O. Hommel Co. v. Ferro Corp.*, 659 F. 2d 340 (3rd Cir. 1981), *cert. denied*, 455 US 1017 (1982); *Malcolm v. Marathon Oil Co.*, 642 F. 2d 845 (5th Cir.), *cert. denied*, 454 US 1125 (1981); *D.E. Rogers Assoc. v. Gardner Denver Co.*, 718 F.2d 1431 (6th Cir. 1983), *cert. denied*, 467 US 1242 (1984); *Henry v. Chloride*, 809 F.2d 1334 (8th Cir. 1987); *William Inglis Baking Co. v. ITT Continental Baking Co.*, 668 F.2d 1014 (9th Cir. 1981), *cert. denied*, 459 US 825 (1982); *Black Gold, Ltd. v. Rockwool Indus., Inc.*, 729 F.2d 676, 683 (10th Cir.), *cert. denied*, 469 US 854 (1984) (dictum); *Pacific Engr. & Prod. Co. v. Kerr McGee Corp.*, 551 F.2d 790 (10th Cir.), *cert. denied*, 434 US 879 (1977); *McGahee v. Northern Propane Gas Co.*, 55 Antitrust & Trade Reg. Rep. (BNA) 818, 826 (11th Cir. Oct. 27, 1988); *International Telephone and Telegraph Corp.*, 104 FTC 280 (1984). *See also* P. Areeda, *Antitrust Law* Section 720'c. (Supp. 1987) for discussion and citations to recent cases.

46. The ability to attack high prices by a dominant firm has been established, at least in principle, in *General Motors Continental N.V.*, OJ L 29/14 (1975) and in *United Brands Co.*, OJ L 29/1 (1976).

47. See, e.g., *ECS/AKZO*, OJ L 374/1, 19 (1985).

48. Article 3, Council Regulation 17, OJ L 13 (1962).

49. Id. at Article 9(3); see also EEC, *Thirteenth Report on Competition Policy* at points 217-218 (1983).

50. Id.

51. *ECS/AZKO*, supra note 47 at 8.

52. Articles 15-16, Council Regulation 17, OJ L 13 (1962).

53. Thirteen Report on Competition Policy, Note 49 supra at 218.

54. In the United Kingdom, a House of Lords decision has indicated that both damages and injunctions may be available to private plaintiffs for violations of Article 86, but that the choice of damages versus injunctive relief would be governed by English law, *Garden Cottage Foods v. Milk Marketing Board* 2 All E.R. 770 (1983). In an earlier case (which involved predatory pricing) an injunction was granted ex parte by the High Court in London against a violation of Article 86. *ECS/AZKO*, supra note 47 at 7.

VI

1. Tribunal de Commerce de Bruges, 3rd December 1971.

2. Tribunal de Commerce de Mons, 8th November 1985.

3. Cours d'appel de Bruxelles, 9th December 1977.

4. *Union Professionnelle des Patrons Boulangers-Patissiers v. S.A. Louis Delhaize*, et al, Tribunal Correctionnel de Charleroi, 7th January 1982.

5. See, e.g., *Fédération Nationale des Unions des Classes Moyennes v. Inno*, Tribunal de Commerce de Bruxelles, 12th October, 1981.

6. *Fédération Nationale des Commerçants en Bières et Eaux de Table v. R.T.D. Eddy*, Cour d'appel de Gand, 8th April 1976.

7. See, e.g., *Negociants en Bière v. Delhaize*, supra note 3 (although the appropriate percentage was disputed).

8. *Fradis v. John Martin Ltd*, Tribunal de Commerce de Mons, 23rd January 1985.

9. *Fédération Nationale des Unions des Classes Moyennes v. Inno*, supra note 5.

10. Tribunal de Commerce de Louvain, 13th February 1973.

11. *Fegarbel v. B.V. Mobil Oil and S.A. Seca*, Tribunal de Commerce de Bruxelles, 4th November 1983.

12. Id.

13. Id.

14. Id.

15. Id.

16. *R.v. Producers Dairy Ltd.* (1981), 50 CPR (2d) 265 (Ont. CA).

17. *R.v. Hoffman-La Roche Ltd*, (1980), 109 DLR (3d) 5, 28 OR (2d) 164, 53 CCC (2d) 1 (Ont. HC), Aff'd (1981), 125 DLR (3d) 607, 33 OR (2d) 694, 62 CCC (2d) 118 (Ont. CA).

18. *R.v. Consumers Glass* (1981), 124 DLR (3d) 274, 33 OR (2d) 228, 60 CCC (2d) 481 (Ont. HC).

19. Pièces de voirie en fonte, reported in Lamy, *Jurisprudence*, No. 133 (14th September 1978).

20. Transports routiers occasionels, reported in Lamy, *Jurisprudence*, No. 141 (22nd February 1979).

21. Gaz industriels, reported in Lamy, *Jurisprudence*, No. 146 (26th April 1979).

22. Vinaigre, reported in Lamy, *Jurisprudence*, No. 153 (18th October 1979).

23. Dipyridamole, reported in Lamy, *Jurisprudence*, No. 211 (28th April 1983).

24. Solutés pour perfusions, reported in Lamy, *Jurisprudence*, No. 229 (12th April 1984).

25. Treillis soudés, reported in Lamy, *Jurisprudence*, No. 246, (20th June 1985).

26. Benrath Filling Station, Reichsgericht 18th December 1931, Entscheidungen des Reichsgerichts, Civilsachen Bd. 134, p. 342.

27. Mineral Water Bottles, Bundesgerichtshof 31st January 1979, WuW E/BGH 1579.

28. Electric Razors, Bundesgerichtshof 6th October 1983, WuW E/BGH 2039.

29. Abwehrblatt II, Bundesgerichtshof 10th December 1985, WuW E/BGH 2195.

30. Grey Green Coaches, Annual Report of the Director General of Fair Trading 1985 at 64.

31. Eastern National Omnibus Co, Annual Report of the Director General of Fair Trading 1986 at 31.

32. Scottish and Universal Newspapers Ltd, A Report by the Director General of Fair Trading on an investigation under Section 3 of the Competition Act 1980, 11th January 1983.

33. London Electricity Board, A Report by the Director General of Fair Trading under Section 3 of the Competition Act 1980, 29th April 1982.

34. Monopolies and Mergers Commission, London Electricity Board, March, 1983.

35. Sealink Harbours Limited, A Report by the Director General of Fair Trading under Section 3 of the Competition Act 1980, 14th October 1987.

36. Becton Dickenson UK Limited, A Report by the Director General of Fair Trading under Section 3 of the Competition Act 1980, 15th June 1988.

37. Monopolies and Mergers Commission, Concrete Roofing Tiles, 18th November 1981.

38. Professor Sullivan has observed that in the late 19th century, "the predatory monopolist became a figure in the national demonology." L. Sullivan, *Handbook of the Law of Antitrust* 109 (1977) (hereafter cited as "*Antitrust*").

39. Until 1986, the Supreme Court's most recent predatory pricing decision was *Utah Pie Co. v. Continental Baking Co.*, 386 US 685 (1967). That opinion has been heavily criticized. See, e.g., L. Sullivan, *Antitrust* at 687 ("One can hardly conceive of an approach better calculated to protect oligopolistic price structures against erosion"); Hurwitz and Kovacic, "Judicial Analysis of Predation: The Emerging Trends," 35 *Vanderbilt L. Rev.* 63, 86-92 (1982).

40. 479 US 104 (1986).

41. 475 US 574 (1986).

42. Relatively few predation cases have arisen in the context of challenges to mergers (as in *Cargill*) or allegations of conspiracies to restrain trade (as in *Matsushita*). The two Supreme Court cases nonetheless provide useful — if not complete — guidance regarding predatory pricing that applies in the more common contexts of monopolization, attempted monopolization, and price discrimination allegations.

    As described in the discussion of United States law in Chapter V, Section 2 of the Sherman Act prohibits monopolization and attempted monopolization. One legal element of each of these offences is unlawful conduct, which may be satisfied by proof of predatory pricing. In addition, and also as described in Chapter V, the Clayton Act, as amended by the Robinson-Patman Act, prohibits price discrimination that may substantially lessen competition. According to the prevailing view, price discrimination undertaken to injure one's rivals (i.e., primary line discrimination) threatens to lessen competition only if it is below cost and if the price-cutter will ultimately be able to garner more than the cost of its predatory conduct by subsequently raising prices to supra-competitive levels.

43. 475 US 574 (1986).

44. Id. at 595-96.

45. Id. at 573-74.

46. Specifically, the Court stated: "It follows from these settled principles that if the factual context renders respondents' claim implausible — if the claim is one that simply makes no economic sense — respondents must come forward with more persuasive evidence to support their claim than would otherwise be necessary." *Matsushita*, 475 US at 587. This continues the Court's recent practice of applying economic analysis to test the plausibility of a plaintiff's allegations of exclusionary conduct and antitrust injury. See, e.g., *Business Electronics Corp. v. Sharp Electronics Corp.*, 56 USLW 4387 (US 2nd May 1988), *affirming* 780 F.2d 1212 (5th Cir. 1986); *Monsanto Co. v. Spray-Rite Service Corp.*, 465 US 752 (1984).

47. 475 US at 584-85 n.8.

48. Id.

49. Id. at 585 n.9.

50. Id. at 589. For this conclusion, the Court relied most heavily on the work of McGee, Easterbrook, Bork, and Areeda and Turner.

51. Id. at 590.

52. Id. at 594 (quoting *Barry Wright Corp. v. ITT Grinnell Corp.*, 724 F.2d 227, 234 (1st Cir. 1983)).

53. See, e.g., *International Telephone & Telegraph Corp.*, 104 FTC 280, 396 (1984) (footnote omitted) (quoting *General Foods Corporation*, 103 FTC 204, 341 (1984) for the proposition that "overly broad efforts to apply these standards may sometimes chill 'the rivalry that is the essence of dynamic competition' by discouraging aggressive price and non-price competition"); and *Northeastern Telephone Co. v. AT&T Co.*, 651 F.2d 76, 88 (2d Cir. 1981), *cert. denied*, 455 US 943 (1982) ("Predatory pricing is difficult to distinguish from vigorous price competition. Inadvertently condemning such competition as an instance of predation will undoubtedly chill the very behaviour the antitrust laws seek to promote.").

54. 479 US 104 (1984).

55. Id. at 109-13.

56. Id. at 116 (quoting *Arthur S. Langenderfer, Inc. v. S.E. Johnson Co.*, 729 F.2d 1050, 1057 (6th Cir.), *cert. denied*, 469 US 1036 (1984)).

57. *Cargill*, 479 US at 117.

58. Id. at 119 n.15.

59. "Although the commentators disagree as to whether it is ever rational for a firm to engage in such conduct, it is plain that the obstacles to the successful execution of a strategy of predation are manifold, and that the disincentives to engage in such a strategy are accordingly numerous." Id. at 121 n.17.

60. Id., citing Koller, *The Myth of Predatory Pricing: An Empirical Study*, 4 Antitrust Law & Econ. Rev. 105 (1971); and Miller, *Comments on Baumol and Ordover*, 28 J. Law & Econ. 267 (1985).

61. *Cargill*, 479 US at 120-22. Since the plaintiff did not allege predatory pricing in the District Court — this issue first surfaced in the Court of Appeals — the Supreme Court reversed the judgment notwithstanding that it may have rested on what would otherwise have been a legally cognizable theory.

62. The seven cases include three cases from the Ninth Circuit, one case from the Sixth Circuit that in part disagrees with the Ninth Circuit's approach, one case from the Second Circuit arising in the context of industry deregulation, and two Federal Trade Commission cases.

63. 570 F.2d 848 (9th Cir. 1977), *cert. denied*, 439 US 829 (1978).

64. In distinguishing the "cost of merchandise sold" from "average variable cost," the court of appeals said that the "cost of merchandise" includes:

costs of spirits and bottling supplies, direct labour costs, indirect labour costs, depreciation on the plant, real estate and personal property taxes, bonds and licences, and warehousing and shipping costs. Some of these items are not variable costs; that is, some are costs which do not vary with output. While materials, direct labour, indirect labour, and warehousing and shipping costs are costs which vary with output, plant depreciation, real estate and personal property taxes, and business licences are considered to be fixed costs because they do not vary with output. Thus, a price which is below "cost of merchandise sold" is not necessarily below average variable cost.

Id. at 858.

65. Id. at 856-59. The Fifth Circuit reached a similar conclusion on this product definition issue in *Bayou Bottling, Inc. v. Dr Pepper Co.*, 725 F.2d 300 (5th Cir.) *cert. denied*, 469 US 1160 (1984).

66. Id. at 855-58.

67. Id. at 856 n.7 (quoting *Hanson v. Shell Oil Co.*, 541 F.2d 1352, 1358-59 (9th Cir. 1976), *cert. denied*, 429 US 1074 (1977)). In addition, although the Ninth Circuit acknowledged that long-run as well as short-run welfare maximization are important, the court ultimately supported the Areeda-Turner view that courts may properly disregard long-run welfare effects because they are so difficult to assess reliably. *Janich*, 570 F.2d at 857 n.9. This is one reason why Areeda and Turner urged adoption of average variable cost (a short-run measure) rather than average total cost (a long-run measure) as the test for predatory pricing. *Contra Chillicothe Sand & Gravel Company v. Martin Marietta Corp.*, 615 F.2d 417, 432 (7th Cir. 1980). (Although the court recognized the great value of a short-run marginal cost standard for determining predatory pricing, the court expressed willingness to consider other factors as well because "Section 2 of the Sherman Act makes no exceptions for cases involving administrative difficulty.")

68. *Janich*, 570 F.2d at 857 ["As implied in *Hanson v. Shell Oil Co.*, 541 F.2d 1352 (9th Cir. 1976), *cert. denied*, 429 US 1074 (1977)], an across-the-board price set at or above marginal cost should not *ordinarily* form the basis for an antitrust violation." (emphasis added, footnote omitted)). Even more explicitly, the Fifth Circuit in *International Air Ind., Inc v. American Excelsior Co.*, 517 F.2d 714 (5th cir. 1975), *cert. denied*, 424 US 943 (1976) contemplated that prices above marginal cost but below a short-run profit maximizing level might be predatory if entry barriers were sufficiently high to permit the price-cutter to recoup the costs of its strategy.

69. See, *Transamerica Computer Co., Inc. v. IBM Corp.* 698 F.2d 1377 (9th Cir.), *cert. denied*, 464 US 955 (1983), discussed infra.

70. 668 F.2d 1014 (9th Cir. 1981), *cert. denied*, 459 US 825 (1982).

71. On remand, the jury awarded Inglis actual damages of US$ 8 051 066 for attempted monopolization, US$ 4 335 333 for price discrimination, and US$ 10 334 000 for below-cost sales in violation of California state law. Since these were alternative verdicts, the Court applied treble damages, less appropriate set-offs, only to the largest of the judgments.

72. 668 F.2d at 1035-36.

73. Id. *Accord*, e.g., *McGahee v. Northern Propane Gas Co.*, 55 Antitrust & Trade Reg. Rep. (BNA) 818, 824-25 (11th Cir. 27th October 1988); *Arthur S. Langenderfer, Inc. v. S.E. Johnson Co.*, 729 F.2d 1050 (6th Cir. 1984), *cert. denied*, 469 US 1036 (1984); *International Telephone and Telegraph Corp.*, 104 FTC 280 (1984).

The court in *Inglis* took exception to the definition of variable costs proposed by Areeda and Turner, however, calling it arbitrary and noting that it includes some fixed costs. The court nonetheless declined to fashion its own definition, reasoning that the proper allocation of costs would vary with the change in output accompanying the price cutting. As a guide to variable costs, the court said the starting point should be to compare costs of production before and after the change in output: "The variable costs would then be those expenses that increased as a result of the output expansion attributable to the price reduction." *Inglis*, 668 F.2d at 1037.

74. Id. at 1034-35.

75. 698 F.2d 1377 (9th Cir.), *cert. denied*, 464 US 955 (1983).

76. Two other significant cases challenging IBM's pricing, product development, and marketing strategies for peripheral equipment are *California Computer Products, Inc. v. IBM*, 613 F.2d 727 (9th Cir. 1979), and *Memorex Corp. v. IBM*, 636 F.2d 1188 (9th Cir. 1980), *cert. denied*, 452 US 972 (1981). In these cases, as in many others, plaintiffs claimed that predatory pricing was coupled with other allegedly predatory activity, involving, e.g., design changes, excessive advertising, or refusals to deal. See, e.g., *Northeastern Telephone v. AT&T*, 651 F.2d 76 (2d Cir. 1981), *cert. denied*, 455 US 943 (1982) (discussed infra), and *MCI Communications Corp. v. AT&T*, 708 F.2d 1081 (7th Cir.), *cert. denied*, 464 US 891 (1983).

77. *Transamerica*, 698 F.2d at 1388.

78. The common feature of these potentially predatory, above-cost pricing strategies is that the defendant reduces prices to below the short-run profit-maximizing level. The Ninth Circuit had previously suggested in *CalComp*, 613 F.2d at 743, that such limit pricing might be predatory.

79. *Transamerica*, 698 F.2d at 1387-88.

80. In two cases decided after the Supreme Court issued its opinion in *Matsushita*, however, the Eighth and Eleventh Circuits disagreed with the result in *Transamerica*, and created a conclusive presumption that pricing above average total cost is lawful. *Henry v. Chloride, Inc.*, 809 F.2d 1334, 1346 (8th Cir. 1987); *McGahee v. Northern Propane Gas Co.*, 55 Antitrust & Trade Reg. Rep. (BNA) 818, 824 (11th Cir. Oct. 27, 1988). *Accord Arthur S. Langenderfer, Inc. v. S.E. Johnson Company*, 729 F.2d 1050 (6th Cir.), *cert. denied*, 469 US 1036 (1984) (discussed infra); *International Telephone & Telegraph Corp*, 104 FTC 280, 404 (1984) (discussed infra); *Barry Wright Corp. v. ITT Grinnell Corp.*, 724 F.2d 227 (1st Cir. 1983); and *MCI Communications Corp. v. AT&T*, 708 F.2d 1081, 1114 (7th Cir.), *cert. denied*, 464 US 891 (1983) ("[L]iability for predatory pricing must be based upon proof of pricing below cost.").

81. 729 F.2d 1050 (6th Cir. 1984), *cert. denied*, 469 US 1036 (1984).

82. Id. at 1057.

83. Id. at 1057 (quoting *MCI Communications v. AT&T*, 708 F.2d 1081, 1114 (7th Cir.), *cert. denied*, 464 US 891 (1983)).

84. 651 F.2d 76 (2d Cir. 1981), *cert. denied*, 455 US 943 (1982).

85. See also, *Southern Pacific Communications Co.*, 740 F.2d 980 (DC Cir. 1984), *cert. denied*, 470 US 1005 (1985); and *MCI Communications Corp. v. AT&T*, 708 F.2d 1081 (7th Cir.), *cert. denied*, 464 US 891 (1983).

86. In *Northeastern*, the court of appeals echoed views that it had previously expressed in *Berkey Photo, Inc. v. Eastman Kodak Company*, 603 F.2d 263 (2d Cir. 1979). In *Berkey*, which dealt primarily with the development and introduction of a new product, the court recognized that it would be unfair, and would undermine important economic incentives, to prevent monopolists from competing aggressively on the merits and reaping the rewards of their success. Such competitive efforts could include innovation and product development, withholding company secrets, extensive marketing, exploiting efficiencies of integration to expand into new markets, or participating in joint ventures where the conduct does not unduly restrain competition. Id.

87. *Northeastern*, 651 F.2d at 87.

88. Id. at 88. While the Court did not declare its presumptions to be conclusive, the reasoning and language of the opinion suggest that the presumptions are very strong. *Accord International Air Industries v. American Excelsior Co.*, 517 F.2d 714 (5th Cir. 1975), *cert. denied*, 424 US 943 (1976) (creating a strong presumption, but with an exception when entry barriers are high). But see *McGahee v. Northern Propane Gas Co.*, 55 Antitrust & Trade Reg. Rep. (BNA) 818, 824-25 (11th Cir. Oct. 27, 1988) (pricing between average variable cost and average total cost constitutes

circumstantial evidence of predatory intent, but to "withstand judgment as a matter of law, a plaintiff must have other evidence, either objective or subjective, of predatory intent.").

89. *Northeastern*, 651 F.2d at 88.

90. Id. at 89. For similar reasoning regarding entry barriers in a non-regulatory setting, see *Adjusters Replace-A-Car, Inc. v. Agency Rent-A-Car, Inc.*, 735 F.2d 884, 889-890 (5th Cir. 1984), *cert. denied*, 469 US 1160 (1985).

91. *Northeastern*, 651 F.2d at 88-91.

92. Id. Other circuits also have questioned the utility of fully-distributed costs as a test for identifying predatory pricing by a regulated firm. See, *Southern Pacific Communications Co. v. AT&T*, 740 F.2d 980, 1006 (D.C. Cir.), *cert. denied*, 470 US 1005 (1985), and *MCI Communications v. AT&T*, 708 F.2d 1081 (7th Cir.), *cert. denied*, 464 US 891 (1983). Although the Seventh Circuit in *MCI* was precluded by factors unique to that case from choosing a short-run measure of cost, the Court made it clear that its opinion should not be interpreted as a rejection of an average variable cost standard. 708 F.2d at 1120 n.55. Nonetheless, the Court opined that in light of the capital intensive nature of the telecommunications industry, total cost standards might be more appropriate than short-run measures for the case before it. Choosing among total cost measures, the Seventh Circuit found that long-run incremental cost (analogous to marginal cost measured over the long run) was preferable to a fully-distributed cost standard of predation.

93. *Northeastern*, 651 F.2d at 90.

94. Id. But see, *McGahee v. Northern Propane Gas Co.*, 55 Antitrust & Trade Reg. Rep. (BNA) 818, 823-25 (11th Cir. Oct. 27, 1988), which draws upon legislative history and Supreme Court precedent for the proposition that average total cost is the appropriate line above which no inference of predatory intent should be permitted. While considering pricing below average total cost to be circumstantial evidence of predation, the Eleventh Circuit requires corroborating evidence of predatory intent before permitting pricing between average total cost and average variable cost to raise a legally sufficient inference of predatory intent.

95. 103 FTC 204 (1984).

96. Id. at 341.

97. Id. at 346-47.

98. The Commission found support for its two-step approach in the writings of Joskow and Klevorick [*A Framework for Analyzing Predatory Pricing Policy*, 89 Yale Law Review 213 (1979)] and Areeda and Turner (III *Treatise of the Law of Antitrust* at 354). The Commission noted that it would be appropriate at the outset to confirm the existence of some evidence raising a legal issue on all three elements, for absent such evidence, the need for further analysis would be obviated.

99. *General Foods*, 103 FTC at 345.

100. Id. at 348-64.

101. Id. at 343-45.

102. 104 FTC 280 (1984).

103. Id. at 403. The Commission suggested that a "significant period of time" would be a period long enough to force equally efficient firms to exit the market.

104. Id. at 404. This aspect of the Commission's test is in accord with the approaches adopted by the Second, Fifth, Sixth, Eighth, Ninth and Eleventh Circuits. *Northeastern Tel.*, supra, 651 F.2d at 88, 91 n.24; *Adjusters Replace-A-Car, Inc. v. Agency Rent-A-Car, Inc.*, 735 F.2d 884, 889-91 (5th Cir. 1984); *Langenderfer*, supra, 729 F.2d at 1056; *Henry v. Chloride*, 809 F.2d 1334, 1346 (8th Cir. 1987); *Inglis*, supra, 668 F.2d at 1035-36; *McGahee v. Northern Propane Gas Co.*, 55 Antitrust & Trade Reg. Rep. (BNA) 818, 825 (11th Cir. 1988). Additionally, although the Third, Seventh and Tenth Circuits adopt no express rule, they consider pricing below average variable cost to be a very useful indicator of predatory pricing. *Sunshine Books, Ltd. v. Temple University*,

697 F.2d 90,93-93, 96 (3rd Cir. 1982); *Chillicothe Sand & Gravel Co. v. Martin Marietta Corp.*, 615 F.2d 427, 432 (7th cir. 1980); *Instructional Systems Development Corp. v. Aetna Casualty and Surety Co.*, 817 F.2d 639, 648 (10th Cir. 1987).

105. *ITT*, 104 FTC at 404.

106. Id. at 403-04. This aspect of the Commission's test is in accord with the approaches adopted by the Second, Fifth, Sixth, Eighth, Ninth and Eleventh Circuits, which either articulate a rebuttable presumption of legality or place on the plaintiff the burden of demonstrating illegality. *Northeastern Tel.*, supra, 651 F.2d at 88; *Adjusters Replace-A-Car, Inc. v. Agency Rent-A-Car, Inc.*, supra, 735 F.2d at 889-91; *Langenderfer*, supra, 729 F.2d at 1056; *Henry v. Chloride*, supra, 809 F.2d at 1346; *Inglis*, supra, 668 F.2d at 1035-36; *McGahee*, supra, 55 Antitrust & Trade Reg. Rep. (BNA) at 824-25 (plaintiff must produce additional objective or subjective evidence of predatory intent for pricing between average variable and average total cost to raise a legally supportable inference of predatory pricing). The Second and Fifth Circuits, like the FTC, make the presumption particularly strong that pricing above average variable cost is lawful. Additionally, while not endorsing any particular rule, the Third and Tenth Circuits have also expressed agreement with the proposition that pricing above average variable cost is generally not predatory. *O. Hommel Co. v. Ferro Corp.*, 659 F.2d 340, 352 (3rd Cir. 1981); *Instructional Systems Development Corp. v. Aetna Casualty and Surety Co.*, 817 F.2d 639, 648 (10th Cir. 1987). See also *MCI Communications v. AT&T*, 708 F.2d 1081, 1120 n. 55 (7th Cir.), *cert. denied*, 104 US 891 (1983) ("[P]ricing below average variable cost is normally one of the most relevant indications of predatory pricing.").

107. *ITT*, 104 FTC at 404. This aspect of the Commission's test is in accord with the approaches adopted by the First, Sixth, Seventh, and Eleventh Circuits. *Barry Wright Corp. v. ITT Grinnell Corp.*, 724 F.2d 227 (1st Cir. 1983); *Langenderfer*, supra, 729 F.2d at 1056; *MCI Communications v. AT&T*, 708 F.2d 1081, 1114 (7th Cir.), *cert. denied*, 464 US 891 (1983) ("[L]iability for predatory pricing must be based upon proof of pricing below cost."); *McGahee*, supra, 55 Antitrust & Trade Reg. Rep. (BNA) at 824. The Ninth Circuit expressly rejects the use of a conclusive presumption of legality for pricing above average total cost. *Transamerica*, supra, 698 F.2d at 1388. The Commission's test also is consistent with the strong (if not conclusive) presumptions of legality which the Second and Fifth Circuits accord pricing above average variable cost. *Northeastern Tel.*, supra, 651 F.2d at 88; *Adjusters Replace-A-Car, Inc. v. Agency Rent-A-Car, Inc.*, 735 F.2d 884 (5th Cir. 1984).

108. *ITT*, 104 FTC at 288-90.

109. For each of the five regional markets involved, the Commission did evaluate the respondent's conduct and intent in light of the price discrimination claims to determine whether there was any primary line competitive injury. *ITT*, 104 FTC at 423-24, 428-41.

110. *ECS/AKZO*, 28 OJ European Communities (No. L 374) 1(1985)

111. Id. at 20.

112. Id.

113. Id. at 20-21.

WHERE TO OBTAIN OECD PUBLICATIONS
OÙ OBTENIR LES PUBLICATIONS DE L'OCDE

ARGENTINA - ARGENTINE
Carlos Hirsch S.R.L.,
Florida 165, 4° Piso,
(Galeria Guemes) 1333 Buenos Aires
Tel. 33.1787.2391 y 30.7122

AUSTRALIA - AUSTRALIE
D.A. Book (Aust.) Pty. Ltd.
11-13 Station Street (P.O. Box 163)
Mitcham, Vic. 3132   Tel. (03) 873 4411

AUSTRIA - AUTRICHE
OECD Publications and Information Centre,
4 Simrockstrasse,
5300 Bonn (Germany)   Tel. (0228) 21.60.45
Gerold & Co., Graben 31, Wien 1 Tel. 52.22.35

BELGIUM - BELGIQUE
Jean de Lannoy,
Avenue du Roi 202
B-1060 Bruxelles   Tel. (02) 538.51.69

CANADA
Renouf Publishing Company Ltd
1294 Algoma Road, Ottawa, Ont. K1B 3W8
Tel: (613) 741-4333
Stores:
61 rue Sparks St., Ottawa, Ont. K1P 5R1
Tel: (613) 238-8985
211 rue Yonge St., Toronto, Ont. M5B 1M4
Tel: (416) 363-3171
Federal Publications Inc.,
301-303 King St. W.,
Toronto, Ont. M5V 1J5   Tel. (416)581-1552
Les Éditions la Liberté inc.,
3020 Chemin Sainte-Foy,
Sainte-Foy, P.Q. G1X 3V6, Tel. (418)658-3763

DENMARK - DANEMARK
Munksgaard Export and Subscription Service
35, Nørre Søgade, DK-1370 København K
Tel. +45.1.12.85.70

FINLAND - FINLANDE
Akateeminen Kirjakauppa,
Keskuskatu 1, 00100 Helsinki 10   Tel. 0.12141

FRANCE
OCDE/OECD
Mail Orders/Commandes par correspondance :
2, rue André-Pascal,
75775 Paris Cedex 16   Tel. (1) 45.24.82.00
Bookshop/Librairie : 33, rue Octave-Feuillet
75016 Paris
Tel. (1) 45.24.81.67 or/ou (1) 45.24.81.81
Librairie de l'Université,
12a, rue Nazareth,
13602 Aix-en-Provence   Tel. 42.26.18.08

GERMANY - ALLEMAGNE
OECD Publications and Information Centre,
4 Simrockstrasse,
5300 Bonn   Tel. (0228) 21.60.45

GREECE - GRÈCE
Librairie Kauffmann,
28, rue du Stade, 105 64 Athens   Tel. 322.21.60

HONG KONG
Government Information Services,
Publications (Sales) Office,
Information Services Department
No. 1, Battery Path, Central

ICELAND - ISLANDE
Snæbjörn Jónsson & Co., h.f.,
Hafnarstræti 4 & 9,
P.O.B. 1131 – Reykjavik
Tel. 13133/14281/11936

INDIA - INDE
Oxford Book and Stationery Co.,
Scindia House, New Delhi 110001
Tel. 331.5896/5308
17 Park St., Calcutta 700016   Tel. 240832

INDONESIA - INDONÉSIE
Pdii-Lipi, P.O. Box 3065/JKT.Jakarta
Tel. 583467

IRELAND - IRLANDE
TDC Publishers - Library Suppliers,
12 North Frederick Street, Dublin 1
Tel. 744835-749677

ITALY - ITALIE
Libreria Commissionaria Sansoni,
Via Benedetto Fortini 120/10,
Casella Post. 552
50125 Firenze   Tel. 055/645415
Via Bartolini 29, 20155 Milano   Tel. 365083
La diffusione delle pubblicazioni OCSE viene
assicurata dalle principali librerie ed anche da :
Editrice e Libreria Herder,
Piazza Montecitorio 120, 00186 Roma
Tel. 6794628
Libreria Hœpli,
Via Hœpli 5, 20121 Milano   Tel. 865446
Libreria Scientifica
Dott. Lucio de Biasio "Aeiou"
Via Meravigli 16, 20123 Milano   Tel. 807679

JAPAN - JAPON
OECD Publications and Information Centre,
Landic Akasaka Bldg., 2-3-4 Akasaka,
Minato-ku, Tokyo 107   Tel. 586.2016

KOREA - CORÉE
Kyobo Book Centre Co. Ltd.
P.O.Box: Kwang Hwa Moon 1658,
Seoul   Tel. (REP) 730.78.91

LEBANON - LIBAN
Documenta Scientifica/Redico,
Edison Building, Bliss St.,
P.O.B. 5641, Beirut   Tel. 354429-344425

**MALAYSIA/SINGAPORE -
MALAISIE/SINGAPOUR**
University of Malaya Co-operative Bookshop
Ltd.,
7 Lrg 51A/227A, Petaling Jaya
Malaysia   Tel. 7565000/7565425
Information Publications Pte Ltd
Pei-Fu Industrial Building,
24 New Industrial Road No. 02-06
Singapore 1953   Tel. 2831786, 2831798

NETHERLANDS - PAYS-BAS
SDU Uitgeverij
Christoffel Plantijnstraat 2
Postbus 20014
2500 EA's-Gravenhage   Tel. 070-789911
Voor bestellingen: Tel. 070-789880

NEW ZEALAND - NOUVELLE-ZÉLANDE
Government Printing Office Bookshops:
Auckland: Retail Bookshop, 25 Rutland Stseet,
Mail Orders, 85 Beach Road
Private Bag C.P.O.
Hamilton: Retail: Ward Street,
Mail Orders, P.O. Box 857
Wellington: Retail, Mulgrave Street, (Head
Office)
Cubacade World Trade Centre,
Mail Orders, Private Bag
Christchurch: Retail, 159 Hereford Street,
Mail Orders, Private Bag
Dunedin: Retail, Princes Street,
Mail Orders, P.O. Box 1104

NORWAY - NORVÈGE
Narvesen Info Center – NIC,
Bertrand Narvesens vei 2,
P.O.B. 6125 Etterstad, 0602 Oslo 6
Tel. (02) 67.83.10, (02) 68.40.20

PAKISTAN
Mirza Book Agency
65 Shahrah Quaid-E-Azam, Lahore 3 Tel. 66839

PHILIPPINES
I.J. Sagun Enterprises, Inc.
P.O. Box 4322 CPO Manila
Tel. 695-1946, 922-9495

PORTUGAL
Livraria Portugal, Rua do Carmo 70-74,
1117 Lisboa Codex   Tel. 360582/3

**SINGAPORE/MALAYSIA -
SINGAPOUR/MALAISIE**
See "Malaysia/Singapor". Voir
« Malaisie/Singapour »

SPAIN - ESPAGNE
Mundi-Prensa Libros, S.A.,
Castelló 37, Apartado 1223, Madrid-28001
Tel. 431.33.99
Libreria Bosch, Ronda Universidad 11,
Barcelona 7   Tel. 317.53.08/317.53.58

SWEDEN - SUÈDE
AB CE Fritzes Kungl. Hovbokhandel,
Box 16356, S 103 27 STH,
Regeringsgatan 12,
DS Stockholm   Tel. (08) 23.89.00
Subscription Agency/Abonnements:
Wennergren-Williams AB,
Box 30004, S104 25 StockholmTel. (08)54.12.00

SWITZERLAND - SUISSE
OECD Publications and Information Centre,
4 Simrockstrasse,
5300 Bonn (Germany)   Tel. (0228) 21.60.45
Librairie Payot,
6 rue Grenus, 1211 Genève 11
Tel. (022) 31.89.50
Maditec S.A.
Ch. des Palettes 4
1020 – Renens/Lausanne Tel. (021) 635.08.65
United Nations Bookshop/Librairie des Nations-
Unies
Palais des Nations, 1211 – Geneva 10
Tel. 022-34-60-11 (ext. 48 72)

TAIWAN - FORMOSE
Good Faith Worldwide Int'l Co., Ltd.
9th floor, No. 118, Sec.2, Chung Hsiao E. Road
Taipei   Tel. 391.7396/391.7397

THAILAND - THAILANDE
Suksit Siam Co., Ltd., 1715 Rama IV Rd.,
Samyam Bangkok 5   Tel. 2511630
INDEX Book Promotion & Service Ltd.
59/6 Soi Lang Suan, Ploenchit Road
Patjumamwan, Bangkok 10500
Tel. 250-1919, 252-1066

TURKEY - TURQUIE
Kültur Yayinlari Is-Türk Ltd. Sti.
Atatürk Bulvari No: 191/Kat. 21
Kavaklidere/Ankara   Tel. 25.07.60
Dolmabahce Cad. No: 29
Besiktas/Istanbul   Tel. 160.71.88

UNITED KINGDOM - ROYAUME-UNI
H.M. Stationery Office,
Postal orders only: (01)873-8483
P.O.B. 276, London SW8 5DT
Telephone orders: (01) 873-9090, or
Personal callers:
49 High Holborn, London WC1V 6HB
Branches at: Belfast, Birmingham,
Bristol, Edinburgh, Manchester

UNITED STATES - ÉTATS-UNIS
OECD Publications and Information Centre,
2001 L Street, N.W., Suite 700,
Washington, D.C. 20036 - 4095
Tel. (202) 785.6323

VENEZUELA
Libreria del Este,
Avda F. Miranda 52, Aptdo. 60337,
Edificio Galipan, Caracas 106
Tel. 951.17.05/951.23.07/951.12.97

YUGOSLAVIA - YOUGOSLAVIE
Jugoslovenska Knjiga, Knez Mihajlova 2,
P.O.B. 36, Beograd   Tel. 621.992

Orders and inquiries from countries where
Distributors have not yet been appointed should be
sent to:
OECD, Publications Service, 2, rue André-Pascal,
75775 PARIS CEDEX 16.

Les commandes provenant de pays où l'OCDE n'a
pas encore désigné de distributeur doivent être
adressées à :
OCDE, Service des Publications. 2, rue André-
Pascal, 75775 PARIS CEDEX 16.

72380-1-1989

OECD PUBLICATIONS, 2, rue André-Pascal, 75775 PARIS CEDEX 16 - No. 44785 1989
PRINTED IN FRANCE
(24 89 02 1) ISBN 92-64-13245-7